The Gospel of Mental Health

Endorsements

The Gospel of Mental Health by Stacey McDonald is a refreshing word for the church as well as for postmodern culture. Her research and reflections eradicate the erroneous myths that irrevocable barriers exist between spirituality and mental health. This literary work takes a systematic approach to identifying various paradigms and praxis of spirituality and mental health. Furthermore, the author identifies the synergy of how they work together toward achieving wellness in individual human beings and in their relationships. This is a must read for anyone who wants to acquire wellness and maintain balance in their lives.

—Bishop Jonathan McReynolds, DMin

Stacey McDonald's *The Gospel of Mental Health* does a masterful job tackling a subject too often ignored in the church—namely, mental illness. Stacey's ability to blend theology with psychology challenges readers to confront their unconscious bias toward the mentally ill and their perspective of the traditional "strong saved Christian." Her raw honesty about her life levels the playing field between the healthy and those struggling to be whole and provides a fresh approach to a subject that often creates shame and a sense of condemnation. This is a book that every Christian, leader, pastor, and counselor should read.

—The Reverend Niki Brown, speaker, life coach, author, and host of IGNITE Women's Empowerment Summit

THE
GOSPEL
OF
Mental
Health

FROM MENTAL HELL TO MENTAL WELLNESS

Stacey
McDonald

NASHVILLE

NEW YORK • LONDON • MELBOURNE • VANCOUVER

The Gospel of Mental Health
From Mental Hell to Mental Wellness

Published in New York, New York, by Morgan James Publishing. Morgan James is a trademark of Morgan James, LLC. www.MorganJamesPublishing.com

Proudly distributed by Ingram Publisher Services.

Unless indicated otherwise, all Scripture quotations are from The Holy Bible, New International Version® NIV®, copyright © 1973, 1978, 1984, 2011 by Biblica, Inc.™ Used by permission. All rights reserved worldwide. Scripture quotations marked NKJV are taken from the New King James Version®. Copyright © 1982 by Thomas Nelson. Used by permission. All rights reserved. Scripture quotations marked NLT are taken from the Holy Bible, New Living Translation, copyright © 1996, 2004, 2015 by Tyndale House Foundation. Used by permission of Tyndale House Publishers, a Division of Tyndale House Ministries, Carol Stream, Illinois 60188. All rights reserved. Scripture quotations marked MSG are taken from THE MESSAGE, copyright © 1993, 2002, 2018 by Eugene H. Peterson. Used by permission of NavPress. All rights reserved. Represented by Tyndale House Publishers, a Division of Tyndale House Ministries.

Morgan James
BOGO™

A **FREE** ebook edition is available for you or a friend with the purchase of this print book.

CLEARLY SIGN YOUR NAME ABOVE

Instructions to claim your free ebook edition:
1. Visit MorganJamesBOGO.com
2. Sign your name CLEARLY in the space above
3. Complete the form and submit a photo of this entire page
4. You or your friend can download the ebook to your preferred device

ISBN 9781631958564 paperback
ISBN 9781631958571 ebook
Library of Congress Control Number: 2021952424

Cover Design by:
Rachel Lopez
www.r2cdesign.com

Interior Design by:
Christopher Kirk
www.GFSstudio.com

Morgan James is a proud partner of Habitat for Humanity Peninsula and Greater Williamsburg. Partners in building since 2006.

Get involved today! Visit MorganJamesPublishing.com/giving-back

To my husband
I learned the definition of love through the Bible. I experienced that love on a spiritual level when I received salvation. I never imagined it possible to share that level of love spiritually and naturally on this planet. But your support, sacrifice, gentleness, prayer, encouragement, and unceasing commitment have lifted love off the pages of the Bible and into every day of my life. I dedicate this book to you.

Contents

The Gospel of Mental Health

I n your mind's eye, take a moment to paint a picture of the way you feel about yourself. The colors you use should represent the quality of your relationships: rich (i.e., fulfilling), dark (i.e., toxic), or shallow (i.e., convenient). The background of your picture should reveal your belief system, such as faith and hope, and anything that antagonizes it, such as bitterness or resentments. Frame that picture with your ability to manage feelings and deal with adversity.

Is the picture you painted something you would place in a prominent room in your home? Or is it something you would put in a horror film?

Is it a picture you would want posted or shared with others?

Does the painting bring you peace and joy, or does it generate shame and embarrassment?

Is your view of your own mental health inspiring or instead more of a frightening mental hell?

You just completed an informal screening of your own mental health. Whatever your initial results may look like, I'd like you to realize a few important aspects of your quick informal screener. First, your picture, as bad as you may have painted it, is only a snapshot of you in the present moment. You have already taken the first step toward changing and repainting your picture by opening up this book. Second, you are not alone in your assessment. Lots of other self-paintings from human beings such as yourself resemble yours in the challenging gallery of life. And third, you deserve to have a beautiful and healthy painting to view through your thoughts and actions.

Mental health is how effectively you are able to live in your own skin emotionally, psychologically, and socially. While it's wonderful to be at peace with others, it really does not amount to much if you cannot be at peace with yourself. After all, you often have a choice as to whether or not you want to spend time with other people, but you have to be with you all of the time. Mental health is the one driving force of your life which affects every critical area that determines the you that you are. If you feel as if your life is even somewhat out of control or going in a direction you really don't want, you can take back the wheel and begin to steer yourself in a mentally healthier direction. With each new page you turn, you can begin repainting your mental picture.

This starts with you realizing that mental health and the gospel of Jesus Christ go hand in hand. "Gospel" simply means good news! There is good news among the sleepless nights, intrusive thoughts, broken relationships, and broken hearts. There is good news for the mental hell that fires the flames of hurt and grief. Within these pages, I will proclaim to you this gospel: namely, that there is hope and help to be found in the timeless and precious Word of God. Our Bible never leaves us in the dark concerning good news for our souls, our bodies, and our mental health. Mental health and the gospel have never been mutually exclusive. After all, there is no mentality that is healthy without God.

Whatever mental health challenges that you're facing will no longer move you to shame but toward a loving God who cares about your mind as much as he does your soul. You may be saved and prophesy like Elijah and dance like King David while speaking in a heavenly language like the apostle Paul—but are you happy? Do you have healthy relationships? Do you sleep in peace? When you look in the mirror, do you see someone that you actually like looking back at you? It is fully possible to lay hands on the sick and witness their recovery after which the healer goes home, closes the blinds, and cries herself to sleep. I know. I have done this.

In *The Gospel of Mental Health*, I will challenge your assumptions and help you be honest with yourself. Through Scripture, I will help you guide your course correction with empathy and encouragement. From the mental battles of Jacob to Esau, King David to Samson to New Testament stories, and right into mental health struggles I have faced and you may too, you will find strategies for coping and calming and finding peace in the hills and valleys of your mental health journey. At the end of each chapter, I have provided a written prayer that will pull on heaven to help champion your mental health journey. In addition, you will find "Journal Jewels" you can use for your personal journal or small group study. These will enable you to dig deeper into your personal goals for mental health and practice the skills you are learning. This book will not only positively impact your mental health, but it will greatly impact your prayer life through conversations with God while showing you how to process your experiences and emotions.

1

Starting Today

Don't put it off; do it now!
—Proverbs 6:4 NLT

A lthough characteristics of healthy living are common knowledge, when it comes to following through with decisions toward long-term health, we often begin with words like "I'll start tomorrow." We know we need to start today, but tomorrow seems to be an acceptable plan and commitment in the moment. The problem is that tomorrow ends up becoming a moving target that we never come close to hitting. As tomorrow moves to the next day, we find ourselves overindulging in the unhealthy because we imagine, "Tomorrow I'll do better." With tomorrow right around the corner, today packs itself with wild oats as if we are storing up for an unhealthy winter. Whether it's eating a tub of Ben and Jerry's ice cream, finishing a pack of cigarettes, or emptying the rest of that bottle of wine, we are fully committed to maximizing our unhealthy today as an illusion of preparation for the over promised and under delivered health of tomorrow. As for all else in our life, we understand that those things must be done today. Bills have to be paid. The situation at work must be taken care of right now. The misbehaving child must be dealt with immediately. But when it comes to decisions concerning our health, we keep putting them off till tomorrow. "Deal with my mental health tomorrow" our sign reads. But when we look at it then, "tomorrow" becomes the next day. Mental health time never comes.

Most of us care more about our physical health than our mental health. We'll go to a gym or buy exercise equipment for the house or go for walks, runs, and hikes. What so many of us don't understand is that mental health and physical health are inseparable. When we take care of our body, we also take care of our mind. After all, "A peaceful heart leads to a healthy body" (Proverbs 14:30 NLT). The opposite is also true: an incessantly troubled heart leads to an unhealthy body. Have you ever been so stressed that your head began to pound, your blood pressure rose, or you experienced muscle tension, digestive problems, hemorrhoids, or hair loss? If you nodded your head to even one of those symptoms of stress, you can relate to the inextricable link between the physical body and mental health. Likewise, if you have ever suffered from such debilitating pain that your mental health became affected, prompting your physician to prescribe antidepressants, then you had yet another confirmation that there's a real link between the physical and the mental.

If you are not experiencing sickness, be advised: just because you do not have a disease does not mean you should not be concerned with your physical health. In order to maintain good physical health, you must exercise and eat healthy regularly. If you don't, you will not have good health for long. The same applies to your mental health. Right now, you may not feel depressed or anxious or be experiencing the unexpected and sometimes painful vicissitudes of life. This does not mean that you should fail to take steps to maintain even your current mental well-being. If you have it, you need to maintain it, or you will not have it for long. You must make a commitment and priority to maintain and strengthen your physical and mental health starting today.

> **Journal Jewel:** What important goals concerning your physical and/or mental health have you put off until the elusive "tomorrow" and why?

Unfortunately, we may not become concerned about our physical health until illness strikes. Once the physician says our cholesterol, glucose levels, or blood pressure is high, we then start watching what we eat and drink and make a much more serious commitment to daily exercise. Tomorrow has officially arrived. We may have previously thought of exercise as something that people do because they have too much time on their hands; but when the diagnosis hits the table, we comprehend the magnitude of the consequences of our personal physical neglect. For some individuals, had it not been for sickness, the importance of maintaining physical health would not have been magnified in their lives. In this regard, even sickness can be a blessing.

Likewise, many people rarely focus on mental health until they suffer from mental illness, such as anxiety, depression, bipolar disorder, or post-traumatic stress disorder (PTSD). Previously, they may have never considered meditation, journaling, balancing work and home life, or processing their emotions. But the moment they realize that their mental life is unwell and adversely impacting their daily living, relationships, work, and spiritual life, then they recognize the importance of mental well-being. Mental illness is a condition that impairs how one thinks, feels, processes, and behaves. Once mental health becomes a mental hell, we are alarmed enough to act. Alarms are designed to wake us up and remind us that there is somewhere we need to be. That somewhere is out of mental hell and into mental health. We can get there, including you!

Journal Jewel: What other areas of your physical or mental health have been affected by what you're putting off? Are you experiencing lethargy, increased work absences, decreased libido, decreased attention span, poor work performance, and the like? If so, how do you plan on changing your current trajectory?

If you have found yourself in an abyss of mental torment, have you ever thought, *God, something must be wrong with my salvation because I am not supposed to suffer depression, anxiety, or (dare I say it) struggle with suicidal ideation?* Although you are saved, you can still experience varying levels of trauma, from developmental to acute, be it sexual abuse, community or domestic violence, bullying, assault, medical trauma, and so on. As a Christian, you may also experience anxiety, dissociation, depression, panic attacks, PTSD, and other mental health disorders. When something goes wrong with the body, we do not normally question our salvation. When something goes wrong with the mind, however, suddenly erroneous fears bellow the lie, "You must not be saved" or "God must not be pleased with you," furthering a downward mental spiral. The shame and secrecy of emotional and mental pain increases the likelihood of tragedy.

If you are among those who feel trapped by not just depression, anxiety, or trauma but also the shame of it, I encourage you to reach out to others despite how vul-

nerable it makes you feel. If you're experiencing a bank-
ruptcy of hope, I admonish you to borrow from someone
else until your refill comes. Reach out for someone trustworthy to take your hand. Whatever you do, don't suffer
in isolation. The strategy of the lion, your adversary, is to
identify the wounded, isolate them, and then attack. We all
need one another. Community is more than a good idea.
God has created us as social beings who need a sense of
belonging, support, and purpose. Community is critical to
our mental health.

I vividly recall the effectual and fervent prayers of the
saints even as a child. For example, when someone was
diagnosed with cancer or lupus or was in a car wreck or
struggled from drug addiction, the saints cried out to God
on their behalf. These prayers of intercession pulled on
heaven. They were prayers that championed for the sick
because they were able to empathize with their plight. As a
young child, I witnessed miracles from these prayers. I will
never forget watching the tumor of one of our church family
members disappear right in the middle of a prayer service.
These experiences strengthened my faith and emboldened
my prayer life to ask God for the impossible—the impossible attached to any physical illness, that is.

I was one of four children blessed to be raised by both
biological parents. My parents met in the local church,
courted, and were married in the church. They were set
to raise their children in the church. However, when my
father was in his late twenties, he started showing symp-

toms of sickness. His behavior changed drastically and in ways I could not comprehend. He once locked me in the closet for singing "I keep falling in love with Him," the opening lyrics to a song we often sang in church. Whoopings were common during that time, but in my home they were unpredictable. I just couldn't tell when, why, or how a "correction" would occur. My father did not drink or use drugs. Something more sinister was changing him from the inside out. His behavior as a father and as a person began to change abruptly. Even his communication skills started to wane. My most vivid memory was seeing him urinate in the middle of the living room floor. At that moment, every idea I had constructed as to how people are supposed to behave was stunned by the man I knew as dad. These were not symptoms related to cancer or some physical disease. Instead they were markers of something that others in our small congregation could not relate to. My dad began showing symptoms of schizophrenia.

If he had suffered symptoms of sudden weight loss, weakness, or a tremor of the hand, those surrounding him would have rushed to support him. But when the mind becomes unwell and behaviors are affected, the common reaction is rejection. Those who prayed for healing in so many other instances demonized my father's affliction. Without ever hearing the term, I witnessed and became a participant of implicit bias. Implicit bias resides in the subconscious. It not only affects how certain people are perceived, policed, categorized, treated as patients, taught as students, or hired and fired as adults. It also affects how we pray for and come to the aid of others.

God doesn't regard us this way. He is impartial in his treatment of us and his love for us. The 'pigs in a blanket' New Testament passage is well known. In order for the Jewish apostle Peter to go and minister to and pray with the gentile family of Cornelius, God had to give him a vision to reveal to him that gentiles (non-Jews) were on God's menu to receive the good news: "God has shown me that I should not call any man common or unclean" (Acts 10:28 NKJV). From that divine message Peter understood that "God shows no partiality" (v. 34 NKJV). This insight gave the apostle what he needed to minister to people he would have never considered before. God cosigned his impartiality by pouring out the Holy Spirit on the entire family of Cornelius after they heard the gospel presentation (v. 44).

Bias dishonors God's will that all humankind be saved, but it also insults the mercy of God by further victimizing the victim. I was no more than four years of age when my social conditioning began to be established, creating a spiritual deficit in what I prayed earnestly for versus what I rebuked. As a child I believed what was assumed by the adults I trusted—that my dad was evil. In reality, my dad had no more control over his sickness than a cancer patient does theirs. But in the minds of so many others, my dad's actions were somehow his fault, as well as the fault of the devil whom he had allegedly allowed into his life. The bias I held affected my dad, but it also deeply impacted me. I grew up feeling intentionally abandoned and rejected when the truth of the matter was that my dad was no longer capable of caring for himself or for anyone else. He needed support, not condemnation. Even without being able to understand his illness, he needed people who could pray for him and encourage him. I can only imagine how different his life and ours would have been with the prayerful support of his community.

> **Journal Jewel:** What bias may you have shown in your prayer life toward certain illnesses or situations, and how will you challenge that bias?

As a child, I remember visiting my father in a mental institution called Eastern State Hospital. I saw others suffering from similar diseases, and I still did not make the connection that this was no one's fault. Looking back (hindsight is always more generous), who in the world would choose to fall completely apart socially, behaviorally, and emotionally in front of their children and wife? No one wakes up and says, "I want to be lonely, homeless, addicted, marginalized, or depressed." Certainly no one rises in the morning to a fresh cup of coffee and says, "I want to exhibit extremely bizarre behavior."

If you are suffering from mental illness, the good news is that you can still be successful. You can still follow your dreams. Do not be so overcome by the diagnosis that you lose hope for your future. God can heal, yes. And God can also show you success, even in sickness. In the meantime, regularly see a physician who shows an investment in your mental health progress. Jesus points out very practically that the sick need a doctor (Matthew 9:12). Ask your physician questions. Advocate for yourself. You are a major part of your treatment. Whatever you do, don't give up. Don't lose hope. If hope is all you have, you have more than enough. Fight on and live.

In regard to my father, over twenty years passed, and we rarely spoke. I spent those years in anger and resentment for "what he did to me," as if he had some selfish motive for unravelling. It was not until I studied psychology that I began to understand, empathize, heal, and reconcile. His illness did not take his physical life so much, but it did cost him his family and other facets of his life. When I look at him now, I no longer see an evil man. I see a man of immense courage and strength to continue to live and smile with a mental illness while simultaneously being rejected, abandoned, and demonized by so many others.

As an adult, I began asking questions relating to my father's Adverse Childhood Experiences (ACEs) and learned he had quite a few factors that put him at greater risk for a mental health disorder. He was raised in a home with domestic violence and substance abuse, resulting in him and his siblings being placed in a group home. His experiences there continued the theme of trauma. The greater the number of Adverse Childhood Experiences, the greater the likelihood of physical, educational, economic, emotional, behavioral, and social problems. And yet, through longsuffering, my dad still holds onto his faith. Yes, a man with schizophrenia and a man of faith. Faith in Christ is not predicated on health, wealth, or social status. Just as there are people of faith with diabetes, cancer, or addictions, or in poverty, middle class, or wealthy, there are people of faith with various mental health disorders. Salvation is available to all and embraced by people from all expressions of life.

The man I vilified is still living, smiling, and enjoying life in spite of every adverse childhood experience, current illness, and past rejection. He still suffers, especially when he does not take his prescribed medication, and that suffering can be as extreme as putting him in a catatonic state. However, daily he fights, desires to be loved, and shows his love for his family and friends. Thankfully, when those who may be well intentioned condemn what they do not understand, God chooses a much better path. He loves us. He loves us all. He loves us without restraint or conditions. He loves us well. He loves us when we are sick. And he does not abandon us based on the category, source, condition, or consequences of our sickness.

The shepherd, musician, and ruler David is perhaps one of the most beloved characters of the Bible. And yet, the man after God's own heart (1 Samuel 13:14) suffered bouts of anxiety ridden with intrusive thoughts (Psalm 6:6–7), depression (38:9), and feelings of worthlessness (22:6). Through it all, God never renounced David but still considered him a man who would follow him (Acts 13:22).

The truth of God's faithful love for those suffering mentally and emotionally is further echoed in 1 Kings 19. The prophet Elijah, whom God used to show miraculous signs and wonders, began to show signs of a mental health disorder. Elijah suffered from depression coupled with loneliness and considered it better to be dead. God did not respond to the prophet's depressed prayer for death with a rebuke, chastisement, or a lecture of how he should not feel that way considering all that God had done for and through him. Instead, God prepared food and drink for him, encouraged him to eat some more, spoke to him in a gentle whisper, and reassured him.

And what about the prophet Jonah? When he prayed to God out of anger, depression, and resentment, God did not call him a devil and remove him from service. Instead, the Lord asked him to consider why he was angry and gave Jonah a practical tutorial about his love for all people so Jonah might better understand grace (Jonah 4).

Not once when mental health becomes a mental hell does God throw more embers to exhibit his displeasure or to further disgrace the afflicted. Instead, he showers his children with comfort as a revelation of his loving grace. I repeat, God loves us well and God loves us sick. And as we work together throughout the pages of this book, God will be with you throughout the journey.

> **Journal Jewel:** Write down some truths you want to speak to lies concerning sickness and salvation.

If you have realized that it may be a good idea to reach out to someone you know is suffering but you haven't because you did not know how, today is a good day and right now is a good minute to check in with him or her. Starting today, be the good Samaritan who was not so busy with spiritual matters that he missed the most important laws of all: "'Love the Lord your God with all your heart and with all your soul and with all your strength and with all your mind'; and, 'Love your neighbor as yourself'" (Luke 10:27).

If you, like so many others, have felt the sting of rejection because of mental illness, reach out. Today is a good day and right now is a good minute to make an appointment with a therapist. It is okay not to be okay, but it's not okay to ignore the tools and strategies that nourish mental health. If you do not build your mental health, the big bad wolf of trouble, sickness, change, loss, heartache, and betrayal will blow and your whole house will come crashing down. These winds will blow regardless of your religious affiliation, skin color, socio-economic status, and pedigree, but they do not have to destroy you. Because you are cut emotionally does not mean you have to settle for an emotional infection. Prevention is better than searching for a cure. Utilize mental health tools and strategies within this book to help keep your wounds as clean as possible until they are healed.

> **Journal Jewel:** What new things are you willing to feed your mental health starting today and why? Write down the start date as part of monitoring your progress throughout this book. You may have implemented a tool that will change your outlook, energy levels, and/or perspective, and therefore your life.

Starting today, feed your mental health! "Don't put it off; do it now" (Proverbs 6:4 NLT). Learn something new!

Enjoy some intellectual candy by doing things that spark your interest in life and living.

Explore new places and cultures.

Try Christian guided relaxation, deep breathing, or meditation.

Never had a garden? Consider planting one. There is a reason the Bible starts with a garden (Genesis 2:8).

Learn how to play a musical instrument.

Challenge your body and your mind with exercise.

Make healthy companionship a priority, and by all means meditate on God's Word.

Starting today, right now in fact, is a perfect time to invite God into your mental health goals.

Holy Spirit, I thank you for speaking to me through each page of this book, for showing me your might, my weaknesses, and my strengths. There are some things I never imagined I would have to seek your face for because there are some problems I never imagined I'd have. I thank you, Lord, for specializing in every issue, pain, and complexity of my life. You are not arrogant. You take all of me in without hesitation or reservation. You guide my footsteps, nourish my thoughts, strengthen my today, and inspire my tomorrow. Lord, I thank you for every trial of my life, from childhood to the present and even those that will come. They have revealed your power to sustain and prosper me. Thank you for bringing me to a place of growing knowledge.

Every physical and mental health goal I have set, I ask that you bless. Every challenge that may arise, I ask that you prepare me to face. And every time I think I am not able, remind me that you are and in you I always am. In the name of Jesus, amen.

2

Intrusive Thoughts

And now, dear brothers and sisters, one final
thing. Fix your thoughts on what is true,
and honorable, and right, and pure, and lovely,
and admirable. Think about things that are
excellent and worthy of praise.
—Philippians 4:8 NLT

It was 1:30 a.m. I started counting, hoping I'd be able to fall asleep again. One, two, three . . . three hundred and one. Number one crept in innocently. Number two without a second thought. Three was somewhat reasonable, but *three hundred and still counting by 1:40 a.m.?*

I stayed awake because of the overwhelming flood of intrusive thoughts. Just ten whirlwind minutes of grappling with these intruders can make you feel like what was only ten minutes of a fight to sleep seems more like days. Intrusive thoughts are in part unwanted thoughts or mental images that can cause and even exacerbate stress and anxiety. These are thoughts so invasive that genuine conscious attempts to change the course of the tide in your mind appear futile.

They can begin with just a question: "How did that even happen?"

Then quickly grow into a storm of "How did I not see it coming?"

Soon your mind whirls with:

- "I wish I had . . . "
- "I should have . . . "
- "I know, I'll . . . !"
- "No, trust God."
- "God help me."
- "What am I going to do?"
- "I can't believe s/he did that to me."
- "I should have said . . . "
- "Next time I'm going to . . . "
- "I wonder how early I can take care of this tomorrow, which is actually today."
- "Hopefully, I won't have to miss work."
- "I may have to miss work."

After going through all of the different scenarios of what else could come of this, you stop and think to yourself, *This is ridiculous. Stop thinking about this. It's 1:52 in the morning!* Unfortunately, what was meant to be a time of rest resembles more of a desperate soul singlehandedly working to fix a dam with a leak. Without a proper plug and expertise, 6 a.m. arrives with the scoreboard reading: Sleep – 0; Intrusive Thoughts – 100.

If this has only happened once in your life, it's one time too many. The ability for your own mind to cause sleeplessness when the body is tired, chaos when the heart longs for peace, or physical symptoms when there is no virus or reason for pain is wickedly uncanny. Intrusive thoughts are just that—unexpected and unwanted intruders that can seem to come out of nowhere. To experience intrusive thoughts is nothing less than going toe-to-toe with a ruthless bully you cannot see and therefore cannot accurately take aim at or disarm. They intrude on sleep, peace, conversation, and even prayer.

There is no physical weapon to defeat it, but it has itself become a weapon. It does not have a measurable weight in pounds, but it feels like a ton of bricks. There is no accurate description of its height, build, or color so you can't call the police and report it. There are no bruises, broken bones, scrapes, or black eyes to describe what it has done. Nonetheless, the fight is on as you toss and turn and throw the covers only to finally give up the fight by turning on the television or grabbing something to eat so early in the morning. Your job still needs you in just a few short hours as well as your spouse, children, and other commitments. Life, work, relationships, ministry, bills, and meetings did not fight with you in the wee hours of the morning. All those things are well rested and expect the fully alert and whole you.

> **Journal Jewel:** List out the intrusive thoughts that are attempting to intrude upon your rest and peace. How have those thoughts inter-fered with your sleep and daily living?

Every race has competitors, from cars to horses to people; but when the mind races, it has no rival except itself. Cars, horses, and people all have lanes and rules to ensure safety and a reasonably fair competition. The mind? Not so much. These intrusive thoughts keep piling up and running over themselves, as they pick up speed and multiply without a finish line in sight.

With a clear picture of this all-too-familiar nightmare, can you calculate just how quickly mental health can become mental hell? Perhaps not in the two minutes from 1:30 a.m. to 1:32 a.m., but certainly during the exhausting torment of nonstop rounds stretching to 4 a.m. and possibly onward until you have to brush your teeth and get ready for work. The danger of this marathon battle is not so much the time in minutes or hours but the intensity of the intrusiveness. A few minutes and maybe even a few hours of anything can be bearable, but when the intensity prevents sleep and forces its way into and against rational thought, it is nothing short of hellish. This is a mentally unhealthy place to be.

However, you have turned the right page to win restful sleep! You do not have to surrender to the bullying of intrusive thoughts. You can win without disappearing from the fight in the abyss of prescription drugs. I am not against medication when necessary; however, I have observed the sometimes hilarious, occasionally embarrassing, and generally unsafe impact of prescription sleeping aids. Sleep is already the most vulnerable state of being. Adding medication that alters behaviors during that most vulnerable state can be dangerous. It is healthier in the long run to learn strategies to overcome thoughts that exalt themselves above your will. It's time to add some strategic weapons to your arsenal and prepare yourself to win this battle so you can take back your rest and your mind.

Winning Strategies

Journaling

One strategy you can use to bring out the yellow paint and create lanes and structure for your thoughts is journaling. Writing out what you are thinking and feeling in order to separate facts from feelings will help you steer your mind down the right path, while dethroning the intrusive thoughts that cannot and will not produce anything positive that you need for the day ahead.

Sometimes stressful situations can be so overwhelming that we have difficulty processing how we really feel or think. That's when intrusive thoughts race in. Journaling will help you process your thoughts and feelings about them by writing them out line by line. You will find that your thoughts are tamed by processing them. Your thoughts need lanes, structure, rules, and order. Otherwise, you'll spend the night herding cats, an impossible feat. While you are writing, it is a good time to record fresh ideas and additional strategies to equip your mind to not just fight but also win.

Mental health is your ability to understand and process information and experiences, while emotional health is your ability to manage and express feelings related to those experiences and information. When struggling with what may feel like a hopeless battle of feelings gone rogue, you may wish you were more of a machine than a human. After all, if you were a robot, you would not be fazed by the stressful situation that has your eyes wide open and your blood pressure rising. Robots are not bothered by betrayal, deceit, loss, layoffs, or relationship problems. Nonetheless, you are fortunate that you are not mechanical. You are human and actually able to feel hurt, confusion, or sadness. Because of your ability to feel those emotions, you also have the ability to feel peace, love, and hope. To feel is a wonderful blessing! But it is vital that we manage our feelings or that blessing can quickly become a burden. Although sadness, confusion, and hurt may be necessary for a season of loss or a situational moment, it is unhealthy for these feelings to intrude during your time of rest since rest will aid in your healing. Having processed your thoughts, experiences, and the emotions related to them, you will be prepared for rest.

Journaling is certainly a great way to process and an effective strategy, but it has one important rule. You may begin with the plight, but you need to end with what is going right (Philippians 4:8). Our minds are excellent artists. Our imagination is perhaps the greatest unknown artist. Its skillful to create images so real to us that we are soothed even though what was imagined was just that, our imagination and not our reality. On the other hand, those images can become so dark or worrisome that they can bring us distress even though they aren't real. Regardless of the somber colors our situations and imaginations may attempt to hand us, we can fix our thoughts to arrive at something as remarkable as grate-fulness, even when we find ourselves in dark places. However, this fixing of thoughts is not on the imagined or fictional but "on what is true, and honorable, and right, and pure, and lovely, and admirable" (4:8 NLT). Upon acknowledging the plight of whatever you may be facing through your journal, seal the journal with what is going right, with some good news, even the Good News! If our thoughts are fixed on only the plight, intrusive thoughts are fueled. But when we fix our minds on what is right, such positives as trust, confidence, peace, joy, and hope come alive. In fact, the number of right things in any of our lives is extensive.

- Consider the fact that you are loved unconditionally and eternally.
- You are also a child of God (1 John 3:1) and one of the "chosen people, a royal priesthood, a holy nation, God's special possession" (1 Peter 2:9).
- Moreover, "neither death nor life, nor angels nor rulers, nor things present nor things to come, nor powers, nor height nor depth, nor anything else in all creation, will be able to separate us from the love of God in Christ Jesus our Lord" (Romans 8:38–39).
- In Jesus Christ "we have redemption through his blood, the forgiveness of our trespasses, according to the riches of his grace" (Ephesians 1:7).
- "And we know that for those who love God all things work together for good, for those who are called according to his purpose" (Romans 8:28).

These items are just the beginning of all the good things that are yours and mine—right now! No matter what else is happening in our world, we have much good we can count on and yes, find rest in.

King David is a prime example that while there may be a lot going wrong, focusing on what is right is not only possible but also peaceable. The Bible describes David as a man who suffered the guilt of a bloody past, rejection from a mentor he longed to please, betrayal from his own son, criticism from the people he served, disparagement from his brothers, and no significant recognition from his father. I firmly believe that a large reason David did not actually lose his mind was because he processed his emotions through writing. His journaling is perhaps one of the most beloved books in the world, the book of Psalms, most of which he wrote. Although many of his psalms began with the woes of his then-present reality, he took out his paint brush, often painted with blues and blacks, and then transformed them into statements of victory, faith, and hope. Through journaling, you will find that your paint brush has the power to create a sense of well-being and optimism that lies beneath a fiasco of fury created by the fears gone rogue in your mind.

As you write out the situation and your insight into it, be sure the lanes do not lead you off an abyss or cliff. You ensure that you'll stay on the path by *directing* your thoughts. Yes, you will have to be your own traffic officer. But I assure that you can direct your thoughts to a safe, peaceful, and positive place. You'll find mind-saving wisdom in Philippians 4:8: "And now, dear brothers and sisters, one final thing. Fix your thoughts on what is true, and honorable, and right, and pure, and lovely, and admirable. Think about things that are excellent and worthy of praise." Your final written thought should reflect at least one of these qualities, even if it is unrelated to your current situation.

Journal Jewel: Have you ever considered that you are the designated traffic officer of your thoughts? And if you do not accept the position, your thoughts will become not only intrusive but darkly invasive. To avoid this consequence, at least once per day practice verbally to begin with the plight but end with what is going right. The words that proceed from your mouth may begin with a complaint but direct it to a place of compliment. When your journal and your mouth both agree, a lifestyle of gratefulness and peace will be nourished and grow.

Beware, there will be times when you are journaling about one situation and another will come to mind. Do not avoid it by trying to ignore its presence. Perhaps the thoughts from that situation which had not been dealt with are what caused the present unhealthy thoughts to gain momentum so quickly. Through journaling you may find a thread that holds both of these situations together, and you may be able to sew something beautiful from it.

Write out what you think and how you feel.

Process those thoughts and feelings.

It is worth repeating: You may begin with the plight but end with what is going right.

Another motivating advantage to the strategy of journaling is the ability to review past entries and find that most of your worries never manifested. This is evidence that incessant worrying causes us to needlessly lose sleep and peace. An extremely small percentage of persons reading this book will revisit their journals and actually find that their intrusive, worry-filled thoughts became a reality (we will discuss dealing with harsh realities in chapter 5). However, the vast majority of you will soon realize that worry does not work for you; it works against you. You did not gain any helpful insight from your night of work (a.k.a. worrying). You put in hours of overtime but did not receive any of the overtime pay for the hours logged. This truth should drive you to journal in order to perform some checks and balances with arguably your most important assets—your mental and emotional health.

Cultivate Stillness

Journaling is an excellent processor, but regardless of how much time and effort you spend doing it, if you have not tamed your mind for stillness throughout the day, your mind will not behave as you want it to at night. When our minds are constantly overstimulated by social media, television, and video games, our brains search for more stimuli when we lie down to sleep. When those stimuli are not available because our eyes are closed, the mind can create its own soap opera or reality TV show.

Prepare yourself for the sleep that awaits and give your mind a fighting chance from the beginning. Before a UFC fight or boxing match, the fighters use critical time before the bout to prepare mentally and physically. You never see a fighter in the locker room watching TV or scrolling on his phone during the hours leading up to the fight, and the same goes for our preparation before we close our eyes at night in our bed. Avoid screen time (television, phone, iPad, laptop, etc.) before bedtime because, although your fingers may have hit the off button on the device, it may not be completely turned off in your mind. Exposure to blue light even two hours prior to bed will make falling asleep more difficult, giving access for those intrusive thoughts to flow in more easily. You may think your chosen device is helping you to wind down, but in reality it is winding you up, the very opposite of rest. Those hard-to-turn-away-from shows from your sixty-inch prized possession or that intriguing gossip from your preferred social media site are more than just entertainment. Blue light emitted by screens inhibits the production of melatonin, the hormone that aids in your ability to fall asleep. Not only does screen time before bed make it more difficult to fall asleep, but blue light also decreases REM sleep, which means more mental fog and less problem-solving and memory storing.

Like the lion mentioned in chapter one, intrusive thoughts look to pounce on you when you are tired. For those who have suffered from intrusive thoughts, you know that when your eyelids close, it's like the bell has just rung to signify that the fight has now begun. Don't be at a disadvantage in the fight right out of the gate. Instead, use the last couple of hours before bed to decompress from the day by unplugging from all media before lying down. This discipline will help you get the rest you need and prepare you for the fight and the much-needed prize of sleep. Instead of screen time, try journaling, reading a physical book of interest, or listening to calming music or to your favorite speaker. The goal may sound simple. However, for those who struggle with intrusive thoughts, these steps will be necessary so that you can get up in the night and return to bed—and back into peaceful sleep— rather than going through a wrestling match in the early hours of the morning.

Jesus instructs us to "not worry about your life, what you will eat or drink; or about your body, what you will wear" because life is "more than food, and the body more than clothes" (Matthew 6:25). And yet, intrusive thoughts are often exactly that—anxious thoughts about the would haves, could haves, and should haves that cause us to miss the moment as we worry about the next.

Two more excellent ways to cultivate stillness and thereby help us master intrusive thoughts are guided relaxation and meditation. For the Christian, these techniques do not involve emptying our mind of all thoughts, escaping from reality, or trying to become one with the cosmos. Rather, the purpose of these two strategies is to pay attention to the precious God-given moment and breathe with an emphasis on setting "your mind on things above" (Colossians 3:2) in gratefulness. These mental health jewels will help guide you in relaxing from head to toe, or toe to head, whichever you prefer. At the end of this book, you will find links to guided relaxation and meditation that will help relax, encourage, center, and empower you as a believer to live in the precious moment rather than in the uncertain future and the often misinterpreted past.

Physical Exercise

Another great weapon against intrusive thoughts is daily exercise. You may have been dreading to hear that, but you should know that exercise has a multitude of mental and physical benefits. Not only does exercise lower blood sugar and strengthen the heart, bones, and muscles, it also releases natural endorphins, and yes, helps to ensure a restful night's sleep. It does all of this without a pill. The endorphins released through exercise act as both a mood booster and a sedative. The bonus is, exercise is absolutely free! It is perhaps one of the most easily accessible and beneficial yet underused treatment for anxiety and depression.[1]

How amazing is it that God embedded a natural solution to sleeplessness and anxiety right into our bodies? God is more than just a Creator; he is our Father. Like a good Father, he has provided for troubled times before troubles come. If there was any doubt in your mind that God is concerned about our mental well-being, the proof is in our very bodies he created. Because of his provision, you don't have to wait until your opponent shows up for you to get into the fight. Preparing beforehand with physical exercise three to five times per week for twenty to thirty minutes will significantly improve depression and anxiety and help you resist throwing up your hands in despair when your mental challengers arrive.

Sweet Blessings

Another thing you can do is train your thoughts on what is good, true, and beautiful in your life.

One particularly difficult night I laid in bed, sorely needing sleep. I had a multitude of tasks to complete the next day and a few fairly big decisions to make that would require a clear and rested mind. With the tasks undone and the decisions not finalized, intrusive thoughts entered during a night where sleep was much coveted. I had already exercised, turned off all screens at appropriate times, and journaled and prayed, and yet my mind's off button was still elusive. So I decided to do what I had watched in cartoons when I was a child, just modifying it a tad bit. Instead of counting sheep, I would ponder each gift in my life for which I was grateful. I began with my ability to inhale and exhale and with the fact that warm blood was flowing through my veins. I walked through each miracle of my ability to see, feel, touch, hear, and smell and then strolled through the wonders of the sea, sky, and earth. Before I could go further, I was sound asleep. No sheep, no counting, just fixing my thoughts "on what is true, and honorable, and right, and pure, and lovely, and admirable." Simply thinking "about things that are excellent and worthy of praise." These saved me from a restless night. Because it is impossible to think more than one thought at the same exact time, fixing my thoughts on the true, the good, and the beautiful was and continues to be my cure.

> **Journal Jewel:** Which strategies are you willing to implement to defeat intrusive thoughts: for example, daily exercise, employing white noise, journaling, limiting caffeine late in the day, avoiding naps, reading a physical book, taking a lavender or magnesium supplement, listening to something positive, practicing Christ-centered guided relaxation and meditation, and unplugging to decompress two hours before bed? Once you have tried one of the strategies, write down the results. (Keep in mind, if one strategy does not work for you, try something different and reclaim your peace of mind.)

Any of these strategies will prove to be helpful, two will be double against your trouble, and applying all of them will transform your life physically, spiritually, and emotionally. If you refuse to wait until you die before you rest in peace, you are reading as a doer and not just as a hearer. As a Christian, talking to God before bed, laying every care before him, and presenting gifts of praise and gratitude are foremost in releasing you to truly rest in peace in this life. Yes, I still journal and meditate as a Christian. King David is a prime example that you can do both.

This is a perfect time to pray and invite the God of rest into your restlessness. After all, the Lord is the source of peaceful sleep: "In peace I will lie down and sleep, for you alone, LORD, make me dwell in safety" (Psalm 4:8).

Father, you said "Come to me, all who labor and are heavy laden, and I will give you rest." I hungrily accept your petition. I confess that I have picked up so many cares and steadied my back to receive the burdens of many others. As if that were not enough, when headlines provoked fear and anxiety, rather than turning off the screens, I shoveled the messages into my mind inciting more unrest. Now I cannot turn off the engine I filled with bad oil. My body is running on fumes, but my mind is fully awake and bombarded by incessant intrusive thoughts.

Help, Lord! Help me to think about things that are true, honorable, just, pure, lovely, commendable, excellent, and praiseworthy as I refuel my mind with the right messages. Father, help me not to worry about anything you are not worried about. I ask that you bless my physical exercise, journaling, self-discipline, and meditation that I may enjoy the bountiful rest they produce and be refreshed to represent your love and grace throughout the day. In Jesus's name, amen.

3

"Just Pray"
Just Isn't Working

The LORD is my shepherd; I shall not want.
He makes me to lie down in green pastures;
He leads me beside the still waters.
He restores my soul; He leads me in the paths of
righteousness for His name's sake.
—Psalm 23:1–3 NKJV

P salm 23 came from the pen of King David. He
had once been a shepherd himself, so he understood firsthand what it meant to say "The LORD is
my shepherd." This psalm gives no hint of David feeling
oppression, intimidation, or coercion at the fact that God
is leading him. Instead, he expresses how beautiful it is to

follow the divine Shepherd. The scenery conveys tranquility born from a trust that does not bend with time or change with seasons.

If you are among the billions of people who have a multitude of responsibilities and others depending on you to do that work, you must know that every shepherd needs the Shepherd. Every king needs the Shepherd. Every CEO, parent, spouse, teacher, doctor, lawyer, principal, custodian, and president needs him. No matter who we are or what we do, all of us need God's caring and loving guidance.

Consider this: If you hold any position of leadership in any capacity, it is imperative to understand that out of all of the responsibilities you have, you are not responsible for the sun rising, the storm brewing, or the rain falling. Take that in for a moment. There is a real peace in knowing that, however high up the ladder you may go, the gravity that causes the ladder to remain in place is not in your hands. Of course, we have responsibilities, but our primary one is to be led by the sovereign Shepherd over heaven and earth. If you forget this, your position of leadership may make you cynical, proud, self-righteous, or even worse. Your high place can create your low place if you forget who is truly sovereign. Satan knows this truth well (Isaiah 14:12–15).

Journal Jewel: Consider the statement "There is a real peace in knowing that however high up the ladder you may go, the gravity that causes the ladder to remain in place is not in your hands." In what ways do you imagine that a daily acknowledgment of a sovereign Shepherd will bring you peace? Have you ever needed reminders of this truth while attempting to shoulder the responsibility of the Shepherd yourself? What was the result?

The Shepherd is the ultimate sovereign, and in his sovereignty he provides as he guides. As David says, "He makes me to lie down in green pastures; He leads me beside the still waters" (Psalm 23:2). His green pastures are evidence of past rain that caused growth and that growth has fed creatures who may have fed you. Still waters are encouragement that eventually the rain will cease and the winds will calm. The rain and winds have their purpose, and so does the stillness. You see, the Shepherd cares not only for people but also dresses the lilies of the field with such splendor that Jesus could conclude about them, "I say to you that even Solomon in all his glory was not arrayed like one of these" (Matthew 6:29 NKJV). And in creating green pastures teaming with life from the microscopic to the grateful full-bellied sheep, God feeds you and me. He graciously adds the bonus of enabling us to perceive the vibrant colors, smells, and sounds of his creation. The Shepherd has done his job. His rain is provision while still waters whisper serenity and tranquility, quietly reminding us that the business around us does not have to keep us busy.

What a beautiful picture our eyes behold of what God has done! But what of the miracles the Shepherd also works that are invisible to the eye? "He restores my soul," David adds (Psalm 23:3). Restoration implies that whatever has been restored needed it. Perhaps the soul had been misused or neglected. Whatever happened to it, the Shepherd takes care to restore the soul, which is the deepest and most vital part of you—the part you cannot dress up to impress or dress down for your comfort. However, whatever its condition, the soul can be restored. Pause for a moment to give God thanks for seeing to your soul's welfare and responding to its need for restoration. It's easy for us to notice when our skin, hair, nails, and even minds need care and renewal. But God goes much deeper into us. He sees what he breathed into humanity from the beginning to create a living soul (Genesis 2:7). One of the greatest benefits of having a relationship with God is to be connected to him as our omniscient Shepherd who knows our needs when we do not. As a reminder of that first life-giving blessing, take a deep breath slowly in through the nose and out through the mouth, and then tell the Lord, "Thank you for restoring my soul."

David then adds that God "leads me in the paths of righteousness for His name's sake" (Psalm 23:3). The Shepherd knows the way to eternal life, holiness, love, joy, and peace. Sheep can be stubborn, and although they have come to know the Shepherd to be trustworthy, they do not always follow where he leads, which brings harm to the sheep and breaks the Shepherd's heart. Jesus, the Good Shepherd, tells the parable: "If a man has a hundred sheep and one of them wanders away, what will he do? Won't he leave the ninety-nine others on the hills and go out to search for the one that is lost? And if he finds it, I tell you the truth, he will rejoice over it more than over the ninety-nine that didn't wander away!" (Matthew 18:12–13 NLT). At one time I was one of the sheep who wandered away only to look up amid the brokenness I created to find the Shepherd reaching for me. I learned something valuable on a personal level: When I lead or follow others without following the Shepherd, crooked is my path. But when the Good Shepherd leads, righteousness is my path. When we follow the leading of the Shepherd, it brings honor to his name because it leads others to him. But because he is good, he does not disown or discard the sheep who stray. Instead, he draws even strays back to him, and he rejoices when we return, for it is not his will that even one of us would perish, which is the certain outcome for the sheep without the Shepherd (1 Timothy 2:3–4).

King David, once a shepherd himself, strikingly illustrates the power, love, and provision of the Good Shepherd in just three verses. Now that we have acknowledged with laudation and thankfulness the grace God gives us daily, I am going to say something that may challenge your perspective: the Shepherd is not guilty if we are failing to experience peace. I will say it again: God is not guilty if we are not experiencing peace.

In the Old Testament, the Shepherd was a guide to his people on the way to the Promised Land. He appeared to his people in the form of a cloud during the day and a pillar of fire at night "so that they could travel by day or night" (Exodus 13:21). God committed himself to be their guide despite their faults, failures, and outright rebellion. As we transition into the New Testament, we're told that "The Word became flesh and made his dwelling among us" (John 1:14). This Word, Jesus, made the proclamation, "I am the good shepherd" (10:11). Jesus's commitment to his sheep does not stop although he knew he would have to die, be buried in a borrowed tomb, rise from the dead, and ascend to the heavenly Father. The committed guidance of the Good Shepherd continues and comforts with the revelation that the Spirit of truth will come and "he will guide you into all the truth" (16:13). The Lord has always been a Shepherd committed to guiding and saving his people.

To guide is the Shepherd's responsibility. To follow is the responsibility of the sheep. Throughout the Old Testament, the Lord beckons his people to follow him and him alone. "It is the LORD your God you must follow, and him you must revere. Keep his commands and obey him; serve him and hold fast to him" (Deuteronomy 13:4). "Keep my decrees and follow them. I am the LORD, who makes you holy" (Leviticus 20:8). When he became flesh and dwelt among us, the instructions to follow him remained unchanged. Repeatedly, Jesus beckons throughout the Gospels to follow him. "Whoever follows me will never walk in darkness, but will have the light of life" (John 8:12). "Whoever wants to be disciple must deny themselves and take up their cross and follow Me" (Matthew 16:24). After the death, burial, resurrection, and ascension of Christ, the Word of God continued the same theme: "For those who are led by the Spirit of God are the children of God" (Romans 8:14).

> **Journal Jewel:** Write down your challenges to following the Good Shepherd. Write how you have or will overcome those challenges.

From the beginning of human history to the present and into eternity, God never stops guiding his people. Likewise, he has never called those who are his to stop following him. Just as important, never has the Lord permitted his people to make any add-ons so as to follow any other way or any other god. Jesus emphatically says, "I am the way, the truth, and the life. No one comes to the Father except through Me" (John 14:6 NKJV). The Good Shepherd laid down his life for the sheep (10:11). We have been purchased by his blood and his blood alone. To this very day, "My sheep hear My voice, and I know them, and they follow Me" (v. 27 NKJV). And when the Lord Jesus comes again, this time descending from heaven with a shout, graves in the seas, mountains, valleys, countrysides, suburbs, and inner cities will break open as even the dead in Christ follow the command of their Shepherd (1 Thessalonians 4:14–17)!

God does not follow any being or anything. He leads. He will never follow our direction. He will always lead. We must follow the Prince of Peace into peace. Our peace is the result of following the right source. Because peace is a result of following, God could not be found guilty when we do not experience peace.

So, for example, when it comes to peace of mind, we will not receive it by simply praying. "Just pray" is not the answer. Prayer alone is not following. In fact, it is perhaps one of the most sedentary actions of our day. If we just pray and do nothing else, we remove all personal responsibility in the matter. We pray for healing and continue to eat poorly and not exercise. We pray for restoration of relationships and continue to hold grudges, have a temper, and reject the notion that we may need to be taught skills for healthy communication. Likewise, many pray for peace and disembowel the peace we do have by following social media asininity, disturbing news stories, and poisonous conversations of gossip or slander. Just praying and then going our own way is not following our Shepherd.

> **Journal Jewel:** Having a responsibility for what we ask for in prayer should not change what we pray for but rather our actions attached to our prayer. Is there anything you've prayed for that you now recognize may require an action step from you?

Free will has given us a choice as to what and who we will follow, and that choice will determine our mental destination. We have a choice to allow society and our own proclivities to lead us to panic and worry, but we also have a choice to allow the Shepherd to lead us to green pastures. Others may throw swords at our peace, but more often than not, we have a choice to leave the sword room like David left the palace when King Saul tried to pin his tail to the wall. Leaving today's sword room may resemble unfollowing or blocking something disturbing on social media or knowing when to turn the channel on the television screen. However, some busy themselves with sword rooms to avoid being alone to process their thoughts, unconsciously believing that they will come out better with a few swords pierced here and there rather than face the truth of who and what they are really following.

Just pray just isn't working because "faith without works is dead" (James 2:26 NKJV). You have a responsibility for what you ask for in prayer. In desperation, a king named Hezekiah prayed to live. In grace, God granted the request and added fifteen more years to Hezekiah's life (Isaiah 38:5). However, Hezekiah took those years for granted rather than for grace. He prayed an effective prayer and yet misused his extended time, resulting in the eventual loss of his predecessors' gains and some of his progeny's freedoms (39:1–7). He just prayed but was irresponsible concerning his answered prayer. Likewise, if we pray for peace and God chooses to answer that prayer, we must not take his gift for granted but act responsibly with it. The apostle Paul gives a list of ways to maintain the peace God gives: Fix your thoughts on the true and honorable, on what's right and pure, and on the lovely and admirable (Philippians 4:8). Fill your mind with the good, the true, and the beautiful that comes from God, and then live accordingly. You will then be following the Prince of Peace.

> **Journal Jewel:** Are there any answered prayers that you may have taken for granted? If so, how do you intend to honor those answered prayers?

Another reason "just pray" just isn't working for many of us is because the disease we are asking God to heal is not something that runs in our families but instead runs in our refrigerators and cabinets. God is able to heal high blood pressure. However, if he does and our diets still include fast food, deli meats, and frozen pizza, we have taken our healing for granted. One of the greatest self-improvement choices I made for myself over three years ago was to become a vegan. I did so after recognizing that during every annual Daniel Fast, I was able to have stressful situations without stressful situations having me. The irritating mind fog and occasional bouts of depression and fatigue lifted during those twenty-one days every single time. I prayed about all of these things many times, but at the end of the prayer, I had a responsibility for what I asked God to do, and I took the challenge. Three years later I am still enjoying the physical and mental benefits of a vegan lifestyle.

We have a responsibility for what we ask for in prayer. Jesus is the Prince of Peace (Isaiah 9:6). It makes sense that following the Word of God would, therefore, bring peace. However, Satan is the prince of the power of the air, and if we constantly expose our ears and eyes to be bombarded with slander, murder, sexual images, and greed, we can expect nothing less than a torment of mental hell after praying to the Prince of Peace. Make it a priority not to entertain foolishness. Whether it be a discouraging word, gossip, or media madness, we are responsible for what we entertain and will reap from it. An impoverished state is a consequence of paying attention to fraudulent words. We must pray for peace, but we must also seek peace, forgive quickly, communicate gracefully, and nourish our ears and eyes faithfully.

This is where prayer can begin the process of change. Perhaps, like me, you never truly considered that you had any responsibility for your mental health. This knowledge should change our prayer and self-expectation. Prayers that were once "God give me peace" followed by no change in behavior or choices may instead begin as prayers of acknowledgement, followed by repentance, supplication, and finally thanksgiving. And once you arise from prayer, next steps should begin which may include counseling, releasing undue stress and negativity, making changes in diet and exercise, and so on.

As the Shepherd never sleeps or slumbers, he is always loving and leading. Let's go to him now with a heart of sincerity and thanksgiving which will move us beyond just pray and into fruitful living.

Lord, I recognize and honor you as my Shepherd. You have given me your Word and your Spirit to lead me. Forgive me for attempting to lead myself and considering you after my mind has become a mental hell. As your servant David said, when I made my bed in hell, you were there to lead me out. Lord, I praise you for this truth. I ask that you continue to guide my footsteps as I recommit to following you and you alone.

Thank you now for the courage to leave the sword room even if it involves leaving the room that held people I desired to have a relationship with. Thank you for showing me the difference between the sword room versus the prayer room and my portion in my transformation. Thank you for the strength to detox from the poisons I have called necessary. I praise you now for green pastures, still waters, for restoring my soul, and for the right path as I follow you. In Jesus's name, amen.

4

With Me Like This, Who Needs Enemies?

Finally, Samson shared his secret with her. "My
hair has never been cut," he confessed, "for I was
dedicated to God as a Nazirite from birth. If my
head were shaved, my strength would leave me,
and I would become as weak as anyone else."
—Judges 16:17 NLT

Have you ever wondered, *With me like this, who
needs enemies?* There is a sense of violation that
comes into play when someone else robs you,
causing logical reactions of installing an alarm system or
maybe carrying mace. But to be the thief of one's own joy,
success, and peace does not yield the same response. There

is no internal reflex of self-defense when the person behind the robber's mask is you. Self-sabotage is the subconscious wherewithal to damage self-success. It may manifest by not completing the final step to a major project, "unintentionally" missing deadlines you knew about and had time to meet, doing something to ruin a valued relationship, or getting everything done and then not showing up to seal the deal. In children this may be their uncanny ability to wait until the last day of their punishment to do something to bring on another reprimand. Each of these behaviors are counterproductive to individual happiness, success, and especially mental health.

As counterintuitive as it sounds, there are various reasons a person may self-sabotage. It may be that a person does not feel as if they deserve success, happiness, or love. It may have never been spoken aloud, but somewhere within is a haunting voice relaying messages of being unworthy that somehow seeped into their belief system and skewed their self-image. The voice may have come from a parent, a teacher, or school bullies, and it may have come as early as last year or even many years before. Whoever and whenever it set itself up within, its unrelenting criticism casts doubt, shame, and false guilt that's capable of eviscerating even the most outgoing and ambitious soul.

I once met a truly intelligent and beautiful young lady who had opportunities for college and internships that seemed to be chasing her down. This young lady self-sabotaged her own success by not completing the simple paperwork for anything offered, although she stated she had a desire for achievement. Just a few sessions of counseling uncovered a gross misunderstanding of the love and grace of God. She had committed a sin in her eyes that was unforgivable, and therefore, even as a young woman who claimed salvation, she continually attempted to punish herself for her sin. Her self-imposed punishment was to refuse to allow herself to progress by self-sabotaging opportunities for her academic and career growth.

I want to stop here and state a truth that you may have never had revealed: You cannot punish yourself for sin. There is a holiness only God owns to punish a soul for sin. As hard as you may try, your efforts will never wipe the slate clean of genuine wrongdoing. No acts of overeating, undereating, procrastinating, cutting, destroying healthy relationships, or refusing to accept scholarships, or even suicide will purge your soul. Only the death of Christ can cover the cost of our sins, and he has taken care of all of them, from the hugely magnanimous sins to what we might think are the most trivial ones (Romans 5:8; Colossians 2:13–15). When you receive his forgiveness by faith, you are forgiven at that very moment and forever. As Paul says, "If you declare with your mouth, 'Jesus is Lord,' and believe in your heart that God raised him from the dead, you will be saved. For it is with your heart that you believe and are justified, and it is with your mouth that you profess your faith and are saved" (Romans 10:9–10). Once God has forgiven you, you can put the knife into self-sabotage and forgive yourself.

> **Journal Jewel:** Is there sin you subconsciously tried to punish yourself for? After reading the following passages, explain why the quest to punish yourself is futile: Romans 5:8; Ephesians 2:8–9; Hebrews 10:11–18; 1 Peter 2:24–25; 1 John 2:1–2.

Although there are billions of people on earth, you are on the mind of God *at this very moment*. You did not have to enter the lottery to win his love. He could never love you any less or any more regardless of what you have or have not done or will or will not do. You have always been loved to death and to life eternal.

The downward spiral in the life of the young lady previously mentioned turned into upward mobility the moment she recognized the relentless love of God. Regardless of her well-intentioned motives, she could never do what only God could do. With an understanding that God's desire to forgive and cleanse us is as relentless this very moment as it was when we first understood our need for his forgiveness, we can receive the free grace of God (Ephesians 2:8–9). Learning more truths about his unconditional love helped show her how to unconditionally love herself, delivering her from present and future self-harm.

Notice, I never mentioned the young lady somehow changing her past. The past is dead weight. There are more people with skeletons in their mind than in their closet, and those in the mind are constantly present while those in closets can be closed in by doors and largely forgotten. In ancient Rome, some criminals were punished by having a dead body strapped to them. They were forced to carry a maggot infested corpse everywhere. They had to eat with it, sleep with it, and even relieve themselves with it. When you attempt to hold on to your past, it's tantamount to strapping a dead body to your mind that will only decompose and seep out poisons that will eventually poison you. You cannot undo what you have done. However, you can manage your actions, starting right now.

For other people, self-sabotage is not rooted in shame but in fear—fear that if they finally reach the height in their dreams, they will fail. The weight of just imagining it is so overwhelming that they may attempt to ensure they never have to face it. It is no wonder Scripture says, "God has not given us a spirit of fear" (2 Timothy 1:7 NKJV). When fear whispers your obituary in your ear and attempts to falsify records about the death of your success and future, recite the plans of the Shepherd, which are to "prosper you and not to harm you, plans to give you hope and a future" (Jeremiah 29:11). Truly we rival the plans of God for our lives when we allow fear to sabotage our success.

Journal Jewel: "Faith comes by hearing, and hearing by the word of God" (Romans 10:17 NKJV). Write and read aloud scriptures that affirm who you are in Christ: such as Psalm 139:1, understood; Psalm 139:13–15, wonderfully made; John 15:13, friends with God; Romans 3:23–24, justified; Romans 8:37, a conqueror; Romans 8:38–39, loved; 2 Corinthians 5:17, new; Galatians 3:13, redeemed; Galatians 3:26, his child; Galatians 4:7, his heir; Ephesians 1:3, blessed; Ephesians 1:4–6, chosen; Ephesians 1:7, free; Ephesians 2:10, his workmanship; Philippians 4:13, strengthened; Colossians 2:10, complete in him.

The Case of Samson

One of the most concrete examples of self-sabotage in the Bible is a man named Samson. He was chosen before he was born to deliver the people of Israel from their enemies. There are some gifts and callings that we never asked for or desired, and yet they are our gifts and our callings. It is important not to mistake God's will for our lives as a suggestion. What we prefer for our own lives will not always agree with our divinely given purpose. And God will not call us to fulfill our purpose when we are ready. Instead, he calls us when *he* is ready. In addition, we may not feel worthy of God's call nor feel up for the challenge, and yet we are called and chosen. Judges 13 reveals the strict requirements

Samson was to abide by to fulfill his divine calling. He was to be set aside to be a Nazirite, and this involved never cutting his hair—not ever. Imagine how heavy that growth must have become and how much that made him appear different from everyone else around him. Samson's difference began before birth and continued throughout his life.

Like Samson, we are all different in one or more ways and that's okay. Maybe you are the introvert called to a place that requires social adeptness beyond your comfort level. You may feel like the only one in the room who is internally buckling while externally smiling and waving. You feel different—and you are.

You may be interested in things that no one else ever wanted to talk about, and if you brought them up, conversations went quiet. You feel different. You are.

Perhaps you were always able to see the other side of the situation and that made others uncomfortable. You feel different. You are.

No matter your difference, God has called you and chosen you to serve in that environment for the space of time you have on this earth.

Don't be afraid of your difference.

Don't panic.

Don't run.

And whatever you do, don't self-sabotage it.

The Shepherd has a purpose for your difference.

One night I wrestled with the reality that, as an evangelist and former pastor, I am yet the poster child for an introvert and have fought through it for years. That night, I heard the Lord say to me, "I made you this way for a reason."

Sometimes the very thing that causes us the greatest grief is what he uses to perform his great power through us. Yes, in our weakness, he is made strong. When I minister before multitudes or witness to just a few, that's one of God's strongest moments in me. Yes, I feel different. Yes, I feel uncomfortable. And yes, I may feel like the exact opposite person to fulfill the call. Still, I am called, and I am chosen. Long ago, I chose to embrace my difference, trust God, and walk it out instead of self-sabotaging the moments and opportunities he afforded me.

> **Journal Jewel:** What is different about you that makes you feel counted out? How has God shown his great strength in the very things you consider weaknesses?

Let's switch lenses for another view. Perhaps your "heavy uncut hair" was in the form of taking on heavy responsibilities early in life that you did not ask for. Maybe it was raising your siblings due to a single-parent household, or maybe your parent(s) had to work multiple jobs. Perhaps you had to care for an alcoholic or drug addicted parent or a parent with a mental illness. Whatever you had to handle, it was a heavy responsibility that you didn't request. It was not fair, but it may have been your responsibility to ensure that you and your siblings were safe. While you may wish you had been called and chosen to another family, that was your different. You are called. You are chosen. And within those heavy responsibilities lies your strength.

Many read the story of Samson as simply being a life of super strength, but his heavy calling meant a life of constant warfare. He was not strong just to be strong. He was strong to fight his nation's enemy. He was stronger than his father and his peers. To whom much strength was given, much was required. His personality may not have matched his calling (like the introverted leader), but by the grace of God he would fulfill his purpose and did. Trust that you can fulfill your purpose too.

Before Samson was born, God promised him success. However, Samson was determined to self-sabotage that success in a quite interesting way. He rivaled the plans of God for his life by sleeping with his enemies. Perhaps he thought, *If I join my enemies, the warfare may end.* Maybe that's not your story. Your story may sound more like *If I put up a wall, I can save myself from potential betrayal or heartbreak.* Or, *If I walk away from Christ, I won't have to fight so many battles.* Or perhaps, *If I do enough wrong things, God will stop calling me.* Regardless of our justification to undermine ourselves and God's plan for us, we can live differently.

I believe Samson's choice in women was his attempt to self-sabotage his destiny. Conceivably he was searching for the woman who would relieve him from the burden of what made him different, and he found that woman in Delilah.

Samson could have cut his hair himself, but then he would have had to take responsibility for undermining his role as a Nazirite and defender of Israel. When a scapegoat is available, it's fallen human nature to put it to use. Remember, when God called out Adam and Eve for their rebellion against him, Adam blamed Eve and Eve blamed the serpent (Genesis 3). Accepting responsibility took a nosedive that day.

When Samson met Delilah, he saw in her a woman who was not just a political sworn enemy (like the other women he slept with), but finally a woman who was not capable of loving him and therefore able to remove the weight literally and figuratively from his shoulders—the weight of destiny, strength, and warfare. He searched for the coldest enemy—an enemy who would remove his burden of being different and cause him to finally be like everybody else. In Delilah, he found that enemy.

Does that sound ridiculous to you? Foolish even? Consider: Have your gifts ever been stifled by the person who claimed to love you—a person who was threatened by your intelligence, calling, and God-given strengths? Is it possible those red flags were glaring and flashing early in the relationship and yet you still went all in? Imagine a person in a toxic relationship with doors miraculously flung open to escape and choose freedom and peace. Has that person been you? Or have you witnessed someone else in such a situation? Did you or that other person walk through the exit sign or remain locked away? Or did they walk out and then into a worse relationship creating a cycle that buried their gifts, or, in Samson's case, buried him beneath falling pillars and rocks? Yes, our choices in relationships, whether friendships, business, and romantic, can work to aid our attempts to self-sabotage against our purpose and our success.

Overcoming Self-Sabotage

As with any problem, the first step toward healing is to recognize it as a problem. Now that we know self-sabotage is an enemy against our purpose, we must be strategic in building our faith. Your words are brick and mortar, perfect tools for building faith. We must speak aloud against the secret fears of being different, the fears of failing, and even the fears of succeeding. Renouncements of fears are not spoken once and then considered done. Rather, they need to be spoken daily against a negative mindset that did not set up residence in your life from a single suggestion. A mindset is shaped over time and therefore takes time to reset. Stay the course, continuing to speak life and positivity even when your mindset is stubborn. Someone told me, "I can't win for losing." My response was, "Then lose until you win!" Whatever the case, don't stop trying.

Now, your actions must line up with your words, which means that it's time to make a plan for the goals you may have suffocated, left to collect dust, or considered only as a figment of your imagination. Your goals may include going back to school, readying yourself and applying for a promotion, public speaking, writing a book, starting a business, becoming debt free, or simply allowing yourself to be loved.

Create a plan that will help you achieve those goals with a reasonable end date. Throughout the process of fulfilling your goals, continue building your faith concerning every gift and opportunity God has given you by speaking life—words of hope and encouragement—to yourself. No doubt, feelings of inadequacy or frustrations will arrive. You are not unique to those feelings. However, not everything that comes to the door is welcome to come into the house. Acknowledge the frustration and sense of inadequacy for what they are—feelings. And then lean on and continue to build your faith, for "Gracious words are a honeycomb, sweet to the soul and healing to the bones" (Proverbs 16:24). Truly, "Death and life are in the power of the tongue" (18:21 NKJV).

> **Journal Jewel:** In the order of importance, with the most important at the top, write out the goals you neglected or rejected. Next to each one, record as best you can what fear kept you from pursuing that goal. Then reflect on how your faith accompanied by action can bring you to finally go after each goal with God leading the way.

If what I've talked about in this chapter struck a chord in your heart, I want you to drink the full glass of the following words: *Be a friend to you.*

As a friend, you likely encourage those around you who are struggling to hold their head up. As a friend, you are likely the loudest cheerleader rooting for their academic, financial, spiritual, and familial success.

Now you must learn to be that compassionate friend to you.

If at any time you feel that you should not reach your greatest potential, as your friend, remind yourself that you are already one of God's "chosen people," a member of his "royal priesthood," a citizen in his "holy nation," and his "special possession." He is the one who has "called you out of darkness into his wonderful light" (1 Peter 2:9).

When fear of failure raises its fist against your goals, recite this truth as a friend to you: "For the Spirit God gave us does not make us timid, but gives us power, love and self-discipline" (2 Timothy 1:7).

When you feel as if you don't have what it takes to get the job done, be the friend that encourages yourself with "I can do all this through him who gives me strength" (Philippians 4:13).

If you ever feel so different that you feel alone in the midst of a crowd, lovingly be that friend who affirms that "The LORD himself goes before you and will be with you; he will never leave you nor forsake you. Do not be afraid; do not be discouraged" (Deuteronomy 31:8).

> **Journal Jewel:** What makes you a great friend to others? Do you ever have a difficult time being that same friend to yourself? If so, why?

Invite God into your places of fear and insecurities as you pray:

My Savior, when you were ready to die for us, you prayed, "Father, into your hands I commit my spirit." Lord, as I am determined to live in you, I pray, Father, into your hands I commit my heart. I can't help but notice how much my heart resembles your hands. Unlike yours, my wounds aren't just from others. Many of my wounds are self-inflicted. And yet, as hopeless as my heart has felt, while in your hands it beats vibrantly, seeing the evidence that it, too, can rise to live again.

Lord, I am amazed that the sight of what you hold does not move you to discard it as damaged goods. The sight of unforgiveness, resentment, fear, hurt, rejection, loss, anger, lust, and jealousy has caused me to not value me. No doubt I have no knowledge of many maladies within me. And yet, with all that I do and do not know, you are fully aware. The psalmist asked, "what is man that you are mindful of him, the son of man that you care for him?" I am convinced from the evidence of your hands, your feet, and your side that the power which raised you will heal my heart that I may use it to love without exceptions and worship without restriction.

The fear that held my heart in terror releases now: fear of failing, fear of succeeding, fears lingering from the past, and fears peering into my future. As my heart is freed from these grave clothes, it leaps and rejoices in your hands. This moment, I renounce every self-attack, self-hate, and self-sabotage. I proclaim with exuberance who I am in you: loved, forgiven, justified, free, born again, redeemed, called out, secure, safe, protected, and saved. Success is my birthright and destiny. I was not chosen by mistake, and I was not called because someone else was absent. I am here on purpose and for a purpose. Peace is my inheritance. Life and that more abundant is my daily grace. Jesus, I give you thanks for these manifold blessings both now and forever, amen.

5

Harsh Realities and Happiness

Give thanks to the LORD, for he is good.
  His love endures forever.
Give thanks to the God of gods.
  His love endures forever.
Give thanks to the Lord of lords:
  His love endures forever.
  —Psalm 136:1–3

A s a school psychologist, evangelist, and former pastor, I have counseled, consulted, preached, taught, and interceded for countless others. Yet, like anyone else, I am not exempt from trouble physically, mentally, or emotionally. Practicing the skills I use to help others continues to be my saving grace in maintaining mental health during tumultuous seasons. And through it all, I have learned that there are certain levels of peace in the midst of pandemonium that no amount of training, psychology, healthy eating, or physical exercise can deliver. During those times, I learned there is a safe dwelling place in God. "In the day of trouble he will keep me safe in his dwelling; he will hide me in the shelter of his sacred tent and set me high upon a rock" (Psalm 27:5). In that place, God may not always command the winds and waves to cease, but he will speak a word that will bring contentment to the heart as the lightning keeps flashing in our storms.

I mentioned harsh realities in chapter 2 and promised that we would deal with them. You know that only an extremely small percentage of our worries actually materialize. I'm referring to the instance when one of those "worst nightmares" you would not wish on your worst enemy truly becomes your reality.

Due to my father's diagnosed schizophrenia, I dreaded the genetic predisposition, which means a greater possibility that other family members would join the 1 percent of Americans who suffer from the disease. What was once a grievous worry became a harsh reality as one of my children was diagnosed with schizophrenia, and it would take every single iota of my faith and more than all of my psychological counseling tools for me to face it. It was a God-sized problem more formidable than anything I'd dealt with before, and God knows I had my fair share of dealings. Its tentacles reached into my peace and happiness and my own overall mental and emotional health. Mentally I had to process the new information and experience, while emotionally I needed to manage my emotions that emanated from the new information and experience.

Journal Jewel: Write out some of the harsh realities you have endured. What do you wish you had done differently to better your mental health during those times?

Rehearsing 1 Thessalonians 5:18, "give thanks in all circumstances; for this is God's will for you in Christ Jesus," has been a part of my daily devotion for over a decade. And yet I struggled to give thanks amid a dreaded and chronic diagnosis. At times I even lost the fight to despair. When that happened, I grasped tightly to fear rather than thankfulness, which further pierced the pain. I looked to the future in doubt rather than thanksgiving as if I were God and knew the end from the beginning. Still praying, I was mentally and emotionally drained and no longer the happy believer I so enjoyed being.

I travelled to Cabo a few months later in an effort to find some semblance of happiness that was tauntingly elusive in my hometown. During this time, I visited an alluringly exquisite resort topped with twenty-four-hour service, perfect temperatures, and a view that resembled one of the grocery store postcards I as a child always assumed were paintings. It was in this paradise that I learned happiness is not found in an address. That opulent tropical dwelling place was perfect to the five senses, but it was not the home of happiness.

While there I witnessed the beach battered by relentless waves. Yet, as unyielding, powerful, and seemingly unchecked as they were, they were under prohibition. They heaved to and fro and yet were begrudgingly constrained by the Creator's harness. God would not allow the water's uncharted depths to overwhelm the earth and consume it. Again and again, the waves pounced persistently, but their gale force was as a light breeze before their Maker. There is a push and pull to waves crashing on the shore, but the pull is stronger than the push, as if God's own hand wrenches them back after their attempt to rush beyond his boundaries.

The ocean is one of God's most beautiful and mysterious creations. And yet within it, and even as a part of its beauty, is the raw and at times brutal nature of it. This part of the ocean was so majestically powerful and absolutely violent that no one was allowed in the water. It was my first time going to a beach without ever being able to tangibly take in the wonders of the water. One couple did not heed the warnings, perhaps unable to see the danger for the beauty, and I watched in horror as the waves almost took them in.

There is no stronger hand than the nail pierced hands of the Lord. No matter how violent the push of disease, loss, or harsh reality, Jesus said, "I give them [those who trust in him] eternal life, and they shall never perish; no one will snatch them out of my hand" (John 10:28). Yes, even Cabo had its own observable harsh realities, but God revealed that he is no less than a good and sovereign God even in the midst of the harshest of realities.

Thankfully, Cabo was not where happiness was for me. Eventually I returned home to face what I had taken a short reprieve from. With gratefulness I learned happiness is not dependent on an address. You may have a house on a hill or a shack in a village. You may be in the unemployment line or in the middle of paradise. The location of any of these things does not determine the happiness of the person there.

God reveals the key to happiness: he inspires his people to be grateful.

Happiness is also not found in the company of others or the lack thereof. A loving spouse will not make you happy any more than being single will make you happy. If you are miserable single, you will be miserable married. If you're miserable married, you'll be a miserable single. Having children is not the antidote to being miserable either, and neither is living your days in solitude.

God reveals the key to happiness by inspiring his people to be grateful.

Happiness is also not found in the delicacies of fine foods or drink, nor is it in the humility of mere scraps on the table.

Happiness is not found in fine furnishings of gold and silver nor in dirt floors and bare walls.

Happiness is not a lack of trouble or responsibilities. You can be happy with great trouble, and you can be happy with immense responsibilities.

God reveals the key to happiness by inspiring his people to be grateful.

By his amazing grace, in the middle of heart-breaking turmoil, I learned what true happiness was. Out of all the Bible studies, prayer times, and counseling of spouses, singles, and children, it was not until I faced a living hell I could not control, erase, or ameliorate that I learned and experienced true happiness. Yes, sometimes going through hell can cause us to appreciate heaven. I found that happiness does have a home, but its home is not made with man's hands, nor can it be torn down by man. The home of happiness is gratefulness.

Notice: since gratefulness unlocks happiness, its lack closes the door to happiness. Some fascinating conclusions flow from this. For instance, it's very possible to love God and be unhappy because you can love God and be ungrateful. The deeper the gratefulness, the deeper the happiness. The shallower the gratefulness, the shallower the happiness.

The key to happiness is gratefulness. And yet people like me travel to Cabo and other faraway places in search of happiness. Others switch spouses to finally be happy. People go into debt to be happy or get hooked on substances in a search for happiness. Others look to sexual adventures, bigger houses, new clothes, dressing up, new hairstyles, and even changing jobs to find happiness. Meanwhile, God's desire for his people to enjoy happiness, to experience joy and cheerfulness of heart, is greater than our own desire for this attainment. When you truly understand God's love for you, you'll find that happiness does not have an expiration date. Because his abundant love endures forever, being grateful for that unmerited love and the grace that accompanies it can bring happiness forever.

Understand, it is impossible for God to have a lack of love. God *is* love—infinitely and forever so! Experiencing a harsh reality, regardless of how awful, does not diminish God's love for any one of us. For God to lack in love is for God to lack in being God. He cannot be reduced, deducted, or degraded. He is eternally who and what he is—God. It is an utterly impossible claim for one to state that a lack of God's love brought on sickness, trouble, or tragedy. God cannot lack in love. Nothing you or I will ever face can be an expression of a lack of God's love for us. He unequivocally and unconditionally loves us forever. And when we are grateful for his eternal love, we can find happiness even in the eye of harsh realities.

Journal Jewel: What have your own personal harsh realities taught you about the love of God that Sunday school, Bible studies, and the preached Word on Sundays didn't?

Insight from Psalm 136

The Creator reveals to his creation the key to happiness. If anyone would have the key to an object, it would have to be its Maker! And we have the Creator's manual! Psalm 136 breathes one refreshing truth twenty-six times throughout and our rightful response to that truth. King David required the priests to recite Psalm 136 during the morning and evening sacrifice as a constant reminder of why we worship the Lord with happy hearts.

This Psalm begins with a command to "Give thanks." To give thanks is to show gratitude in a verbal or physical gesture that rises from the heart due to kindness shown, mercy given, beauty wrought, sustenance provided, or simply because of who (in character or attributes) one is. It is impossible to be grateful and unhappy. Likewise, it is impossible to be happy and ungrateful. Without asking how our day was or how we feel, the psalmist says, "Give thanks!" And this we are to do regardless of the day's events and our mental understanding and processing of it, and regardless of how we feel about it emotionally. The offering of giving thanks to God is always in order.

Verse 1 of Psalm 136 continues: "Give thanks to the Lord" who knows the heart and whether the gesture is genuine or performance. There are times we say thanks out of duty rather than sincerity, while at other times our thanks is before a crowd but not in our heart. And yet the Lord who searches the heart knows the sincere from the spurious. This same Lord is to be the central object of our thankfulness. He is the One who never ceases in kindness, mercy, mighty works, holiness, and righteousness.

Whenever we attempt to make ourselves the center of attention, mental hell follows. For instance, if you've ever suffered from depression, have you noticed that depression is extremely self-centered? What we believe created the state of depression generally ends in "me": what they did to *me*, what did not go right for *me*, who left *me*, what hurt *me*, when it hurt *me*, why it hurt *me*, and, of course, "Why *me*?" Emotional hells stem from three centers of attention that all come from the same person: me, myself, and I.

In contrast, thanksgiving, worship, and praise all take the focus from self and lavish it on the One with the most extreme exchange policy. "To console those who mourn in Zion, to give them beauty for ashes, the oil of joy for mourning, the garment of praise for the spirit of heaviness" (Isaiah 61:3 NKJV). When we place honor and the center of our attention where it is due, God in turn fills our hearts and minds with blessings. The psalmist was onto a breakthrough here, and if we follow his lead, we will begin to exit the hellish emotional pit that self-focus helped create.

Let's delve deeper back into Psalm 136:1. "Give thanks to the Lord, for he is good." He is always good. His goodness requires no outside support. It doesn't need our help or any other assistance of any kind. God is good in an unlimited way. He is good without a beginning of goodness or an end of goodness. He is all good and nothing but good through and through in all his ways. When I think of his goodness, my soul responds in thankful gratefulness. The one who thinks on him will give thanks because of him and for him. If our thinking is right, we should always be thankful. We cannot give on God's level, but we can return to him what is clearly appropriate: our deep and abiding gratitude.

The psalmist finishes verse one, as he does the next twenty-five, with a resounding reminder. "Give thanks to the Lord, for he is good. His love endures forever." His love enters as a shining beacon into the dark tunnel of human failure, mistakes, and ingratitude, and exits that same tunnel without losing any of his light to the darkness. His love passes every test of sin we could imagine putting it through and endures through it all. It endures forever. He is good. His love endures. What a relief!

Journal Jewel: Scripture says that the Lord will "console those who mourn in Zion, to give them beauty for ashes, the oil of joy for mourning, the garment of praise for the spirit of heaviness; that they may be called trees of righteousness, the planting of the LORD, that He may be glorified" (Isaiah 61:3 NKJV). Doubtless, you have already had the Lord make at least one of these exchanges in times past. Write them down here as a reminder that what he has done before, he can certainly do again.

Thankful in Struggle

Understanding these truths about God removes the yoke of self-importance. That idol of an island called self that says things like "You wouldn't understand what I'm going through" and asks such questions as "Why me?" That self doesn't grasp the fact that countless others have endured whatever that self may be facing. The truth is, "There is nothing new under the sun" (Ecclesiastes 1:9). All creatures struggle.

Fish swim unaware as birds swoop in suddenly.

As ants toil, they are stepped on without intent attached.

When rain ceases, so does the vigor of the flower.

The bird cares for her young, and yet its nest may be emptied by a single storm.

Every living thing is in a struggle, and yet every living thing continues to fight to survive and thrive. The fish continue to swim upstream; the ant keeps gathering; flowers don't cease to hope for sun and rain; and birds continue rebuilding and mating. Even the waves behold all the other waves fail to overcome the earth, but they do not surrender or lose vigor. Nay, they fight with the same tenacity as the first, the billionth, the trillionth, and so on. Look closer and you may too observe that every wave when it breaks seems to explode with a shout and leap of hallelujah! These created things seem to know by nature and instinct that life must go on and that it must go on with a praise. It is not our problems that make us unique, but the way in which we respond to them.

May our suffering release a song of gratitude.

May our worst nightmares become our launching pad for thanksgiving.

May our personal hell yield our greatest happiness.

Mind you, I was not thankful *for* the trauma that felt like it was hurled from hell and into my family, but I learned to be thankful *in* it. The apostle Paul concurs with the psalmist, saying "give thanks in all circumstances; for this is God's will for you in Christ Jesus" (1 Thessalonians 5:18). I was not thankful for what my family faced, but somewhere between the weeping, worshiping, and grieving, I learned to be thankful in it. Today, I am not thankful for the diagnosis which continues to create uncertainty and pain, but I am thankful for the certainty of God's love and grace in it. The Covid-19 pandemic, political unrest, and natural disasters all around the world are not circumstances that we may give God thanks for; but as we navigate daily through each challenge, we can all give God thanks for his love, mercy, and grace even while we are living through and facing those challenges. Likewise, Job did not give thanks *for* the loss of his loved ones, but somewhere between his weeping, worshiping, and grieving, he learned to give God thanks *in* the tragedy and loss. For those who have children, you understand that there is nothing that assaults your child which does not feel like it has assaulted your very own soul. And yet, the soul is God's. The soul is therefore comforted by breathing thanks to the One who breathed life into it.

Journal Jewel: Are you going through anything right now that you may not be thankful for but that you can give God thanks in? If so, write a few lines offering him praise and thanksgiving.

Our Limits and His Ways

When present happiness is choked out by arrows of doubt aiming at your future, ask yourself a few questions.

- How can you know that physical, mental, and/or spiritual disease will win when you don't even know the ocean depths?
- How can you know that the trouble will only worsen when you don't know the span of the universe?
- How can you predict the future when you cannot predict which way the wind will blow?

You claim (not by your words but by your worry) to know that darkness, disease, and trouble will make a ruin of you or your family, but you don't even know your next thought, let alone what tomorrow will hold or when the Lord will return. You are not the sovereign God.

His ways are not our ways (Isaiah 55:8). I came to realize that attempting to figure out his ways could make me lose mine. His thoughts are above ours and thankfully will not condescend to our unbelief. If God's thoughts ever condescended to our unbelief, our loved ones would remain lost, no miracle would come, and no deliverance had. Thankfully, our worry does not hinder his work. It does, however, hinder our peace, happiness, and overall well-being. The Bible tells us not to worry, not for his sake but for ours.

If what you may have worried about actually has the audacity to manifest into a harsh reality, you will soon find as I did that life still goes on. And it can go on with happiness, peace, and victory. Whatever your harsh reality may be, it is not the end of the story. You will get through this the same way you triumphed through previous tumultuous storms. It may not be easy, and it will certainly require prayer, meditating on God's Word, a self-care plan, and perhaps counseling, but life will continue, and you can experience happiness through gratefulness in the middle of it all. Your harsh reality may not be the same as mine, but your prayer must be just as real as the reality you face. Let's take a moment to invite God into the storm.

Lord, my emotions as of now have been driven by winds rather than being rooted in who you are and your enduring love. I repent for my lack of gratefulness. Forgive me for my poor memory. It sometimes wells up as springs of joy in remembrance of your works, and other times it stomps off empty of any consideration of you at all. I am sorry, Father. Even in my most heart-wrenching and seemingly unbearable trials, I am compelled to look up with grateful tears and thank you that you did not give me what I deserve.

Now I ask, Lord, create in me a grateful heart. Give me an understanding of who you are. May gratefulness flow from that heart and into every interaction, thought, response, motive, and emotion. I desire sincere and genuine happiness so that my family, coworkers, and friends will have a living witness of what understanding your goodness does. As a believer, it is my desire for my life to paint a picture of a great big "Thank you, Lord." As your love endures, so help me to endure.

And now, Lord, I thank you for hearing and answering this prayer. I love you too.

6

In Pieces

We are the clay, and you [Lord] are the potter.
We all are formed by your hand.
—Isaiah 64:8 NLT

Pulling something apart can bring at least two different emotions. For instance, for me there is enjoyment in pulling Play-Doh apart with my granddaughter—pulling one piece in opposite directions to create two pieces, then four, and so on. This play engages only two of the five senses but in such a pleasurable manner. Perhaps the pleasure is in knowing the pieces will be brought back together, to once again be whole and tucked away in its specifically designed container until the next time.

While watching a program on the Animal Planet channel, I observed another pulling apart: one animal tearing apart another animal. I watched peeking through my fingers due to the "nature" of it, all the while knowing it was exactly that—nature. Unlike the Play-Doh playtime, there would be no putting the pieces back together again. The brutal finality brought a whole new perspective to being pulled apart.

Much like the hunted animal, there are times we may feel as if the pieces of our lives could never come back together again. But you are much more like the first example than you realize. The Bible says, "We are the clay, and you are the potter. We all are formed by your hand" (Isaiah 64:8 NLT). You may feel like you are now in pieces, but with the help of the Potter, you can be put back together again.

The culprit of our erroneous belief that the trauma or circumstances will leave us forever in pieces is called worry. As a verb, *worry* or being overly anxious is related to one animal using its teeth to seize another animal by the throat in an effort to tear it apart. Jesus emphatically repeats the words "don't worry" four times in Matthew 6:25–34. The meaning of the Greek word for "worry," *merimnaó*, means "drawn in opposite directions." When used figuratively, it means "to go to pieces." Jesus recognized that there are times we may feel as if we are going to pieces and therefore warns us against the temptation to worry. Musical artist Bobby McFerrin may have been inspired by what Jesus said when he wrote the song "Don't Worry, Be Happy." One of the song's lines recognizes that in life each of us experiences trouble but adds that worry doubles the trouble. It reminds me of working with Play-Doh, pulling one piece in opposite directions to create two pieces, then four and even more.

Have you ever looked back at something that consumed you with worry and wondered, *How did I let my worry get this big?* In fact, if you were to look honestly at the situation and then look at the worry, you'll likely realize that your worry grew bigger than the situation. You may have initially dealt with the situation with a healthy mindset. As a matter of fact, you may have even dealt with bigger issues before and been proud of how you were able to hold it together. Kind of like when you set a treadmill to go at a certain speed with a certain incline for a certain number of minutes because you feel as if you've conditioned yourself well enough to handle it. Then on one perhaps ordinary day, you begin the same routine. But you reach close to the midway point and then realize that you're not even half-way there and you already want to stop. Similarly, worry finds a way of creeping in when you realize, *I've been at this already for some time. I thought I could handle it. I thought I was strong enough; certainly, I've been through worse before, and yet this still isn't over and I'm more than winded.* You may have been sick for a while, but your illness has not subsided. Maybe it's been a few weeks since your job interview and yet no one has called you back. Or the court date you thought would bring peace only brought another court date. Your child's behavior continues to decline, and now you are feeling your mental health declining. You may be wondering why they even call it mental health because it sure doesn't seem to want to stay healthy!

Worry is not necessarily activated by large events in our lives. It can be the smallest of things that begin an emotional avalanche into a whirlwind of worry.

Jesus on Worry

In Matthew 6, between Jesus repeating "don't worry," he gives reasons we should trust him instead. Jesus points out the Father's loving care for the birds of the air without anyone else's assistance and then asks, "Are you not much more valuable than they?" (v. 26). He mentions the flowers and how they have never taken classes in sewing and never had a job and then adds, "Yet I tell you that not even Solomon in all his splendor was dressed like one of these. If that is how God clothes the grass of the field, which is here today and tomorrow is thrown into the fire, will he not much more clothe you—you of little faith?" (vv. 29–30). Truthfully, you and I should not worry about anything that God is not worried about. And (excuse my English here) God ain't worried about nothin'.

Having ministered using these verses on numerous occasions, I will share something embarrassingly ridiculous with you that I asked God about while frustrated with my own worries. This was not my most shining moment.

My question didn't even concern a harsh reality. Rather, it was over a new ball game, and I didn't have the ball nor did I know the game. But I did have God, and he had given me every reason to trust him from past experiences and regardless of the novelty of the situation. So I looked to him while the worry was tearing me apart and asked, "God, you mean I have to trust you in *everything*?" Perhaps you have been there, you wanted to secure the best lawyers money could buy. You wanted to tap into every resource you had. You wanted to do it your way. And God simply says "Stand still and see the salvation of the Lord" (Exodus 14:13), at which point you may have thought, *God, I've got this one* or *God, you mean I have to trust you in everything?* Your everything may look like a new problem on the job, plus a situation with your child, plus a marital problem, plus a health problem, plus all the other stuff you already laid at the foot of the cross. Whatever list your "everything" may include, the Lord's answer to you is the same as it was to me—a resounding "Yes! Trust me in everything!"

Journal Jewel: God desires for us to trust him in everything. Which thing out of your "everything" have you held in your lap rather than laid on the altar? What would be the difference physically, emotionally, and spiritually if you decided to surrender it to the Lord?

The things we worry about may not be able to be fixed with a few dollars, a Band-Aid, a kiss, or human intervention. But part of worrying means I think that somehow I can fix it. So I pray, and then I worry. I tell God about it and then spend hours throughout the day trying to figure out different loopholes so that *I can handle it*! When God says, "Trust me," and we refuse to trust him, every loophole we scramble for will become our gallows that further strangle our faith and double our trouble.

There's a much better way. Trust God with the problem and refuse to worry about it. Repeat after me: "I will not distress over things that are outside of my control. Once I pray, it becomes God's opportunity and a birthing point of patience and greater faith for me. I free myself from the unattainable goal of being God."

And hear me, God is fighting for you! Any parent understands that you fight the hardest when you fight for your own children. That being said, imagine how passionate God is about fighting for you. You are his child, and he is passionate about fighting for you!

When the Father tells his children not to worry, he is telling us to go against what we once were: unbelievers who were estranged from him. Jesus emphasizes that worries "dominate the thoughts of unbelievers" (Matthew 6:32 NLT). But "Dear friends, now we are children of God" (1 John 3:2). As a pre-salvation condition, unbelief was a lifestyle that many of us embraced most of our lives. It's easy to fall into something that we have become well acquainted with and more accustomed to. And yet the Lord is telling us to allow the new creature we are to do the *faithing*, including when the old creature gets anxious in the waiting. After all, it is trusting Christ that sets the believer apart from the unbeliever.

Consequences of Worry

The Lord has us lay all our cards on the table as he asks, "Can *all* your worries add a single moment to your life?" (Matthew 6:27 NLT, emphasis added). We rarely have just one worry because worry reproduces. Even rescue plans we produce out of worry produce more worries: What if this doesn't work? What if things get worse? What will this mean for the future? When counseling students with anxiety, it's never just one specific worry. For example, their worry about speaking in front of the classroom leads to them worrying that they might make a mistake, which leads to the worry if it will cause laughter, which leads to the worry of whether anyone will sit with them at lunch, which leads to the worry of whether they will be lonely, and these worries often project into their future, creating storm clouds that threaten their future relationships and their thoughts about their future well-being as their worry produces more worries. If our faith is not increased, worry will not die but multiply! It multiplies itself even as it subtracts from its victim physically, emotionally, and spiritually. In multiplying, not only are relationships and sleep disrupted, but blood pressure is raised while the defense of our immune system is lowered.

Despite the damage anxiety can cause, we often lay at the altar situations such as addictions, cancers, and unemployment, while we hold on to worry, leaving it to harm us through its own cruel devices. Worry has become such a normal everyday practice for many believers that it is second nature. We generally worry about what we truly care about. Perhaps that's why it feels so natural. I have never worried about anything I did not deeply care about. For instance, I have never worried about a basketball game or the Derby. You could honestly say, I would not worry so much if I did not care so much. But we would also not worry so much if we truly trusted God's care for us so much. Yes, worrying contradicts the very command of Christ. It may feel "natural" to worry, but worry is the sin against self that is committed without the allure of pleasure. Worry is self-imposed flagellation whereby we inflict emotional and even physical pain on ourselves. We were never meant to become comfortable living in worry. As much as it may feel like second nature, worrying is not natural, and it can be defeated.

My granddaughter was born premature. Before she could come home from the hospital, she had to drink a certain amount of milk daily because if she did not eat, she would not grow, and it is dangerous not to grow. Likewise, worrying hinders our spiritual and relational growth. Worry seeps into our prayer and meditation time with God. We grow spiritually when we meditate on the Word and spend time in his presence through prayer. But how can a heart be nourished by the Word when the mind is occupied with worry? How can one pray effectively when the mind is captured with cares? If you are not eating, you are not growing, and any living thing that is not growing is dying. By the way, my granddaughter, who is now two years of age, cannot stop eating or smiling. She is also at the one hundredth percentile for height and weight. If worry has hindered your growth, do not give up or give in! You can still trust! You can still grow!

Not only does worry hinder spiritual growth, but it also stunts the growth of relationships. If you are a current or past worry champion, you know that someone can be in a full conversation with you and yet you miss everything they said because your mind drifted to various worries. Now stop for a moment and think about having to deal with an issue with your child or coworker after a session of worry. Did you handle it well? After an unplanned date with worry, how was your love life? The last time worry made you deaf in the middle of a conversation, how do you think the other person felt?

In the meantime, the worry that impacts so many areas and levels of our daily life is inconspicuously silent to everyone else. Worry is a silent killer, but its silence is its muscle. It's vying for your attention, shouting frantically while pulling you away from the present and into a fear-concocted future that has not happened. If others could hear it shouting, perhaps someone would muffle its mouth. Instead, the outward silence strengthens worry's inner hold. Its hold will remain until the only one who can hear it actually exposes it.

Shining the light on worry to expose it for the self-defeating weapon it is, is the first step to overcoming it. Certainly talking through your worries with someone you trust is an effective way to expose it, but it's okay to get creative. One of the members of our church shared an effective way her family chose to expose worry. They made a faith box with the top velcroed on and placed it on a top shelf of their coat closet. Anytime she, her husband, or teenagers had a worry, they'd write the worry down, pray over it, and place it in their faith box as a sign that they handed it over to God. But if at any time they began to worry about that thing again, they would have to go and retrieve the worry until they were willing to surrender it again. This served as a sobering reminder to each of them of how tempting worry can be and yet how useless worry is. Perhaps this should be a practice for many of us. I imagine there are many trips I would have made to that box at certain times in my life that would have helped me recognize, expose, and deal with the worries plaguing me.

Overcoming Worry

Through Prayer

Prayer is how we communicate with God. And while we can pray in a variety of ways, I highly suggest that when you cast your worries in prayer, you pray aloud. When we pray silently, worry can sweep our train of thought right off its tracks. If you have ever been on your knees praying silently and stopped praying to go take care of something you remembered during that silent prayer, you have become a victim of your prayer time being hijacked. It is important to pray aloud. David describes his prayer life, saying, "I cry aloud to the LORD; I lift up my voice to the LORD for mercy" (Psalm 142:1). When you are actively talking, it is nearly impossible to think about anything other than what you are talking about.

Physiology helps us understand the benefits of vocal prayer. When talking, the Broca's area of the brain is turning thoughts into spoken words. The Broca's area connects to the motor cortex relaying information to the muscles of your face, mouth, tongue, lips, and throat as to the right movements to form speech. A band of nerves joins in the goal of communication that are dedicated to help you form words and speak clearly. All the while, the part of the brain known as the cerebellum is engaged in helping to open and close the mouth. All of these intricate workings occur simultaneously. Because of this, when you are actively speaking, anxiety and worry must take a back seat. So if you no longer want to become distracted in prayer by worry, praying aloud is the answer. Also, as an added benefit, when the kids or spouse actually hear you praying, they are less likely to interrupt and more likely to mimic this more effective communication with God in their own prayer lives.

Through Listening and Journaling

Now that you know how important speaking aloud is to our communication with God in prayer, it's equally important for you to balance that communication. Whenever we are communicating, it is imperative to allow God time to speak. During your prayer time and meditation on the Word, take time to listen with a pen and paper at your side as you journal. Similar to vocal prayer, when you are actively writing, the mind is so focused on the writing task that mental distractions (including worry) are less likely to occur. We may think of writing as a simple task, but while writing, your brain and body perform a host of complicated assignments that require your mind to pay attention. As you write, three nerves connected to the hand are controlling its sensory and motor functions. Within the frontal lobe of your brain, the motor cortex takes responsibility for the action of writing. The motor cortex partners with other parts of the brain to judge the distance from pencil to paper, the amount of force needed to be applied, which muscles need to be used, and more. The temporal lobe of the brain makes what you're writing memorable to you, which further benefits writing down what God is speaking during prayer and meditation. The frontal lobe of the brain also assists with judgment, reasoning, problem-solving, and planning—all required while writing. It's no wonder that writing is an effective and important way to keep the mind focused and therefore worry-free.

So much of the brain and body are used in positive ways when we pray aloud and write what we hear God speak through the Word and prayer. God created all of these critical pieces to work together when we intentionally speak and write; and yet if not utilized, the marble-sized amygdala, which generates fear and anxiety, can interrupt the process and play a major role in pitting the emotional brain against the cognitive (or thinking) brain. When the amygdala wins, anxiety falsely persists as if you were in real danger. Anxiety attempts to hijack the same parts of the brain that are used to help us remain calm and collected. With the help of the Holy Spirit, praying aloud and journaling help take back control so we can utilize the brain as the gift it was meant to be rather than the weapon of worry it can become.

> **Journal Jewel:** With what you now know about the benefits of praying aloud and journaling what the Lord speaks, what additional meaning and purpose do you think the following verse has for worry and prayer in general? "I cry aloud to the LORD; I lift up my voice to the LORD for mercy" (Psalm 142:1).

Spiritually we help fight against anxiety by prayer and journaling as we meditate on the Word of God. But for those who may feel as if their life is in pieces, just as the term *worry* suggests, there are practical steps to bring the pieces back together again.

One Piece at a Time

Foremost, I encourage you to take worry one piece at a time. Begin by identifying and defining what some of those pieces of worry are. For instance, you may identify that you have an estranged relationship with a loved one. *Estranged* can be defined as ceasing to have a connection with that loved one or at least experiencing a less friendly connection.

Having identified and defined the piece, start with some questions designed to map your plan for bringing that piece back together again. For instance, Romans 12:18 says, "If it is possible, as far as it depends on you, live at peace with everyone." *Is there something I can do to get that piece back together to benefit from obeying this scripture and reconnect with my loved one? There is a gap between me and my loved one. What can I do to shrink or eliminate that gap?* The answers, of course, are as wide as the scenarios that caused the separation. Nonetheless, you will be amazed at how simple the answers could be to those questions when worry is not clouding your thoughts: your reconnection tool could be a text, a phone call, or having a cup of coffee together. Something simple can pull that piece much closer to becoming a whole and fruitful relationship again.

For those family relationships that have become estranged due to misunderstandings, restoration may still be possible if desired. Whether you are like Jacob or Esau, the culprit or the victim, communication is key if the pieces are ever to come back together again. When our feelings are truly hurt, we sometimes want the answers to our hurt to be as complicated as our feelings. Thankfully, that is not always the case. Although communication may sound like too simple of a solution compared to our complicated feelings of hurt or worry, steps to reestablishing communication can be the beginning of wholeness.

When considering options for communication, do your homework as to how that person might be feeling, what is important to them, what makes them happy, and what things they enjoy. This information gives you the ability to choose the right action items that will show your vested interest in reconciliation. For instance, if they are a Patriots fan, an action item might be to go to see a Patriots game with this person. Week by week choose an option to connect and communicate. Set up a weekly phone call reminder to touch base or establish lunch meetings to gradually eliminate the gap. This week your action might be to call the individual. Next week you may choose to offer an invitation to grab a bite to eat together. The hurt or damaged feelings will not be healed in one setting or after an apology, but consistent, planned, and healthy communication over time provide healing balm on wounds that serve to foster reconciliation. Week by week you will likely find that the pieces that seemed irreparable will, like the Potter's clay, come back together again.

After a few months, you can look back and see the practical work put in and the impact it made. There is perhaps nothing more satisfying than to track your progress toward making whole again what had become divided. You may be dealing with just one piece among a hundred others, but if you resolve the matter, you'll at least know that the pieces can actually come back together, one piece at a time. Some pieces may take longer than others to make whole again, but as long as you are making progress, you are in the right position for peace in your fight over worry. When we can actually do something about what we are worried about, worry is irrational.

> **Journal Jewel:** What action items might you choose for something you are worried about? Don't forget to track your progress!

Heart Hurt

As you may have noticed, you will have to take some active responsibility in bringing the pieces back together. If the piece is a divorce, then the responsibility that you take may be more internal than external. A broken heart and what feels like a broken future will require internal wholeness. This wholeness cannot be given by another person, a new relationship, a new car, or a new house. This wholeness will require an action plan for the mending of the heart.

After a divorce, many divorcees feel as if they have no one else, especially if they have defined themselves by their marriage. They can experience shame and guilt due to broken vows regardless of how they were broken. Now more than ever, you need to pray aloud and meditate on the Word of God with a pen in hand. In meditating on the Word, you will find that the Lord is closer to you now than you may have ever realized: "The LORD is close to the brokenhearted and saves those who are crushed in spirit" (Psalm 34:18). The marriage may have failed, but God's love for you will never fail: "For I am convinced that neither death nor life, neither angels nor demons, neither the present nor the future, nor any powers, neither height nor depth, nor anything else in all creation, will be able to separate us from the love of God that is in Christ Jesus our Lord" (Romans 8:38–39). His "plans to prosper you and not to harm you, plans to give you hope and a future" (Jeremiah 29:11) will always remain too.

Along with prayer and meditation, you may also consider therapy. "Where there is no counsel, the people fall; but in the multitude of counselors there is safety" (Proverbs 11:14 NKJV). The claims of worry are often fabricated or completely unfounded. It is difficult to counter the claims of worry when they remain in your head. It's far better to talk about them, to bring them to the light. A counselor can help you deal with them, acting as a wise friend. "As iron sharpens iron, so a man sharpens the countenance of his friend" (27:17 NKJV). Talk therapy is chemical free, and it's an effective treatment for anxieties that may arise from living a new normal, such as a divorce, change in career, or the loss of a loved one.

In the meantime, it's also important to strengthen healthy platonic relationships you may have. Unfortunately, it's easy to neglect healthy relationships while we are dealing with injured relationships. Instead, we need to strengthen what we have left. In fact, I advise that you invest in healthy platonic relationships rather than attempt to form a new romantic one. Because sharp edges can be dangerous, it's best to first begin putting the pieces back together before reaching for something new.

From Self-Help to Other-Help

Let's shift gears and discuss how you can help someone else win over worry. If you have a loved one in a battle with worry, they may not realize that their private battle is showing up in public. Anxiety does not produce cool, calm, and collected people. It does, however, produce complaining, criticism, and contention. Anxiety is internal, but many of its symptoms are external.

Teens, especially, may not realize they are suffering from anxiety. When symptoms show (and they will), it is up to the adult to patiently learn what is weighing heavily on adolescents' minds, although teens may not realize that something is. If your teen seems to have become short-tempered, is sleeping more often, appears distant, or has difficulty focusing, avoid going into authoritative parenting mode and instead be the calm and reassuring voice to help bring them and their pieces back together again. Ask about their friendships, relationships, bullying, schoolwork, and deadlines. Try to determine if they are concerned about anything happening physically (such as hair, pimples, weight, and height) or other insecurities that may be weighing on their minds. It may be none, some, or all of these things. You will not know unless you ask, and they may not even realize it themselves except when you ask.

Because anxious thoughts tell only their own side of the story, talking through those worries with your teen will help reveal truth and hope by exposing "magnilying" glasses. Magnilying glasses are the glasses of worry that magnify lies, such as:

- Things will never get better.
- I can't do this.
- It's hopeless.
- No one will ever like me.
- I'm not good enough.
- I'm not smart enough.
- I'm not attractive enough.

Journal Jewel: Has worry been giving you "magnilying" glasses? If so, talk through worrisome distortion with someone you trust, and write down truths to help correct your false vision. Remember, "Where there is no counsel, the people fall; but in the multitude of counselors there is safety" (Proverbs 11:14 NKJV).

Since children may not always feel free disclosing their feelings to a parent, you may encourage an arrangement for them to reach out to a pastor, counselor, mentor, or trusted loved one so that they, too, can take steps toward being free from the barbs of worry. Being vulnerable enough for any of us to disclose what we truly care about can be uncomfortable. However, there is healing in caring conversation. Simply exposing what was hiding in the recesses of the mind to the light of caring conversation can help bring the pieces back together again. Opening up can be scary, but that same openness will foster wholeness.

The Invitation

The Lord has given us a standing invitation: "Come to me, all you who are weary and burdened, and I will give you rest. Take my yoke upon you and learn from me, for I am gentle and humble in heart, and you will find rest for your souls" (Matthew 11:28–29). If you have prayed about lust and the Lord has brought deliverance . . . if you have prayed about unforgiveness and the Lord made your heart tender . . . if you have prayed about trouble and the Lord strengthened you and brought you through it . . . why would you not boldly bring worry to the One who has provided rest for your soul? Because the Lord has given us free will, he does not just take from us what we do not offer. We must go to him freely and ask.

The Potter says come.

The Father says come.

The Great Physician says come.

The Burden Bearer says come.

Are you weary? Are you burdened by the worries of life? The Lord does not look upon you with an arrogant heart. He shares his character, saying, "I am gentle and humble." He invites us to replace the yoke of worry with his overflowing love and care.

You may feel as if you're in pieces, but you are not damaged goods. You are valuable right now just as you are. Yes, even in pieces. The Potter has never considered discarding you, leaving you, or throwing his hands up in frustration over you. In fact, his specialty is to create masterpieces from broken pieces.

Thoughts of worry, despair, and frustration come and go. You are not your thoughts. You are his possession, his child, his son or daughter, his beloved. You are his masterpiece. As much as you may feel like you are not, he has you and will not let you remain in pieces forever.

Lord, casting my cares upon you feels almost impossible when I care from the depth of my heart. So, Lord, I give you my whole heart and lay it on the altar. For there are no fatalities from the table of the Great Physician and no mistakes from the Potter's wheel. O Lord, have your way with every piece of me. I have never felt so safe as when in your hands. I may not even know where each piece of me lies, but you are all-seeing. You see the piece of me that was pulled apart years ago, and you never lost sight of it. You see the tug of war I lost against my

*thoughts and the carnage from it. Even as you reas-
sured me not to worry, I did. I worried boldly and
without ever considering your will for my thoughts.
Lord, I am sorry it took me so long to bring this
piece of me to you. The worries seemed more of an
appendage than a burden I carried. Now, here they
are, God. All the things I truly care about and the
worries that hover in my mind and heart over them.*

*I see now that you care more about these loved
ones and issues than I ever could. I sit still now as I
feel your nail scarred hands piece me back together
again. The worries for my children, you pick up each
one as if they are precious in your sight. The health
worries, you hold them with tender care. The worries
for the future, you now gather in love. I am but clay,
and these cares were added to my frame by my need to
control what has or may happen. O Potter, I relinquish
all control back into your hands. Make me whole.*

*What relief now as I feel your hand molding
and shaping me. The rest my soul has longed for
is right here with me even now because you are
here, with me, even now. Tears of gratefulness fill
my heart that the lion of worry roared but could
not destroy me. Because of your power, wholeness
is on the way. Jesus, your yoke is my rest. Help me
continue to learn from you as I continue to give you
all of me. In the name of Jesus, the One I love, I
commit my worries and life to you. Amen.*

7

Full of It

Get rid of all bitterness, rage and anger, brawling
and slander, along with every form of malice. Be
kind and compassionate to one another, forgiving
each other, just as in Christ God forgave you.
—Ephesians 4:31–32

Every vessel has its limit concerning how much
it can hold. Just a few more seconds of pouring
past the fill line can cause a mess regardless of
the container's size. Depending on the substance, there
may be more elbow grease required to clean it up, and
the job may be dangerous. Depending on the temperature
of the substance, anything that fell victim to the spillage
may suffer pain and scarring. The substance in the vessel

would have been less likely to spill had some of it been released before adding more. Certainly, when the illustration changes to the vessel as human and the substance as offenses, the effects are just as real and painful and far more reaching. It matters not who you are, my friend; you can only take so much.

Because every person has limits, it is imperative for each of us to process and release and do so frequently. Physical obesity can cause stroke, coronary heart disease, high blood pressure, sleep apnea, fatigue, and more. Similarly, obesity of unresolved issues, such as offenses, also yields symptoms that disturb sleep, decrease energy, and even cause decline in our overall well-being. As painful as the symptoms are, emotional obesity can be healed. Sleeping, breathing, living, and loving will be enhanced if we determine to lose the weight by dealing with the offenses.

When we choose to hold what should be released, the increased volume makes it heavy to carry. We then put ourselves at risk of spilling it all onto unsuspecting bystanders. Family gatherings during celebratory occasions, such as Thanksgiving, Christmas, and family reunions, can turn into a civil war because at least one person was full to the brim and no one else, perhaps including the vessel, had a clue that a spill was on the brink. To be emotionally full is an inward condition. The person's hair and clothing may be well manicured, but no one is able to look inside to see that the person is full of it. All it may take is for a comment to add to the volume, and then "it" begins to spill all over the place. Now what was full of it and spilled overpowers all of the planning, time, and effort of what was meant to be an event to facilitate bonding.

When this happens, the children are left wondering what's happening. The adults are questioning, "Where did *it* come from?" You may look at the person and think, *Wow! I never knew that loved one had it in them*. Or perhaps when it's all said and done, you look embarrassingly in the mirror and think to yourself, *I never knew I had it in me*. The target of the attack genuinely announces, "All I did was ask about how the new relationship was going." Witnesses agree with the statement. But the one who spilled *it* all over the place received much more than the posed question. They kept records of all the other times they had a perception of feeling demeaned by the asker. Their tally is full of the times the target did not think to apologize for small things. Their record of feeling slighted by the target is full. Their tolerance level is full, and then out "it" comes. "I'm done with *it*! *It*'s over!" Only until the reality of the overreaction settles in does the vessel admit, "I didn't mean *it*."

Surprisingly, it's not uncommon to be full of it. *It* can be identified as offenses that have accumulated as unresolved issues. The offense is a perceived insult, rudeness, or some other intentional or unintentional lack of respect. The offenses build inside until they cannot be contained any longer.

You cannot continually tuck offenses away as if they will disappear. Even if time passes and you feel as if you forgot them, it may only take one word or action to bring at least one of them out of hiding. Jesus warns us that "offences will come" (Luke 17:1 KJV). The conditions that lead to offenses coming will vary. There will be times the offender truly had pure motives or was simply naive to his or her behavior. Other times, a person may hit below the belt, so to speak, to intentionally hurt you. Regardless of the motive, if the occurring offense remains unresolved, "un's" are sure to follow: *un*forgiveness, *un*kindness, *un*professionalism, *un*controllableness, *un*raveling, and so on.

Handling Offenses

Smiling while you're offended is not the antidote for offense. It may allow you to save face, but it will not save heart nor keep "it" from continuing to fill up. On the other hand, getting even with a well-thought-out comeback will not ease an offense either. You can, however, learn how to deal with offenses.

One key component to dealing with offense is recognizing your own vulnerabilities and biases. *Why have I given this person the power to frustrate me? Is there history with this person that has been unresolved? Is the person a stranger, but their race, gender, or orientation causes me to be defensive when I otherwise would not have been? Could I have some things I am dealing with completely unrelated to this incident that is skewing my perspective over what was said or done?*

Journal Jewel: When you are already irritated, it's easy to sweat the small stuff. Do yourself and others a favor and give yourself a time out. What kind of things could you do during a self-given time out (for instance, remind yourself of your favorite sermon, song, or Bible passage; take deep breaths and count backwards from ten; hum your favorite song)?

You may be thinking, *But the offender is clearly the problem, and here you are asking me to look in the mirror.* While it may be true that the one who offended you is a problem, the offending person doesn't need to be *your* problem. He or she doesn't have to be the one who pushes you over your edge or causes your "it" to spill over and affect innocent people. My friend, people only have emotional power over you when you allow them that power. You may have made ordinary people into potentates by allowing them influence over your emotions. They never asked for the position, but you gave it to them, and only you can take it back.

Journal Jewel: Emotionally, people only have the power over you that you allow. Can you identify people you have given power to? Write down the power you have given them. Seeing it in writing takes it out of your head and heart and brings it out into the open so you can see it more objectively. Now write how you will take that power back, such as by listening to understand, empathizing, praying for them, or reminding yourself that you have a power that cannot be taken (Acts 1:8). These steps will re-empower you. They will also give you ways to respond thoughtfully rather than hastily when other offenses come.

A change in perspective may just change your outlook, clearing your window of any debris of misconceptions. When you have had a bad day and have said or done things that you would not ordinarily do, such as raise your voice or snatch the receipt away from a cashier, once you're calm you may remind yourself, *I did that because I was having a horrible day. I wouldn't have normally responded that way. In other words, if I had not been turned down for the promotion, ran out of gas on the freeway, left my coffee on the kitchen table, misplaced my keys, received dreaded information from my doctor, or had a falling out with a loved one, I would not have responded that way.*

Unfortunately, when we have had a really bad day, so do those who are closest to us: children, spouse, and coworkers. Even an unsuspecting cashier can get caught in the wake of our outburst. Nonetheless, we can allow ourselves some latitude of mercy because we know our personal situation and how it attributed to our spilling over on someone else. We may also consider how the empathy we apply to ourselves may be applied toward our offenders. Could it be that, just like us, perhaps they're having a really bad day too and need prayer, a kind response, or a rational, calm discussion?

An Error to Avoid

The tendency to overemphasize the behavior of others as deficits or character flaws and to underemphasize our own behaviors as explainable and therefore ultimately excusable is called "fundamental attribution error." People have the tendency to situationally explain away why they may have yelled and snatched the receipt. However, when another person does the same, their behavior is attributed to a personal character flaw or deficit, such as:

- He is a mean person.
- She is a disrespectful person.
- They don't care about anyone but themselves.
- They act like they have had no home training.

But remember when the shoe was on your foot, you were simply having a bad day that led to regrettable behavior.

Journal Jewel: Name some ways that fundamental attribution error has given you peace regarding your behavior while excusing you to give others a piece of your mind. Yes, this is confession time. Empathy is more easily worn when we first remove our masks.

Recognizing our own cognitive bias toward others helps shift our view. Again I ask, is it possible that the interpretation of the person's behavior as offensive was due to the person's gender, skin color, clothing style, relationship status, or any other external factors? The shortcut to making a judgment about what type of person someone may be is sometimes based on an experience with someone else who looked like them or from what was generalized from media depictions. This can lead us to misinterpret behavior and find an offense where one was never meant. Feeling offended requires energy. Could it be that energy was unduly wasted because of perceptual distortion brought on by bias? For some people, the level of energy involved is capable of moving a thirty-three-thousand-pound diesel truck that can likewise produce black smoke emissions that cause cancer, heart and lung damage, and air pollution. Imagine all that energy causing all that damage for a misinterpretation due to cognitive bias! The way we view things (our perspective regardless of how accurate or inaccurate) has everything to do with how it affects us. Getting to know our bias is a proactive step to decreasing offenses.

Journal Jewel: Have you ever found that you unintentionally kept a record of offenses? What actual mental and emotional pros and cons have you experienced from keeping this ledger? Did it make you feel light or peaceful or in control or energetic and happy? Or did it create diesel smoke that caused you and others to feel bad? Be honest with yourself.

A Christlike Response

If after you have considered your own bias in assuming what kind of person someone is based on their behavior rather than on what they may be going through situationally and you still believe someone's behavior was intentionally malicious and without extenuating circumstances, then understand that they are all the more in need of prayer and an uncharacteristic (Christlike) response. We sincerely pray for people suffering from cancer, trauma, and grief. Why would we not genuinely pray for those who may have a negative disposition or poor temperament (be it assumed or otherwise)? Yes, pray for the offending person. Even if their intent was hurtful. You cannot control the actions of others, but remember, "If it is possible, as far as it depends on you, live at peace with everyone" (Romans 12:18). These are more than just wise words; they are the map to living a fulfilled and peaceful life. Drink this counsel daily. If we are going to be full of something, let's strive for *it* to be healthy and life-giving. Besides, what more life-producing words are there than the Word of God? Adding these ingredients into our lives brings an overflow of fragrance rather than something foul. Rather than being over *it* because we have had *it* with him or her, release *it* by giving that person to Christ through prayer.

What positively or negatively brings a change in our behavior is likely to have a corresponding impact on others. If we can change our view, we can change our attitude and prevent the buildup of misconceptions, misunderstandings, and offenses. The bonus is, we save innocent bystanders who would have been otherwise negatively impacted by our neglect of self-management. When we intentionally "get rid of all bitterness, rage and anger, brawling and slander, along with every form of malice" (Ephesians 4:31), we are then empowered to "be kind and compassionate to one another, forgiving each other, just as in Christ God forgave you" (v. 32).

Maintenance Living

Many of us are great at getting rid of negativity by detoxing and decluttering our lives at the annual revival or during men's and women's empowerment conferences, but there are also many of us who are pitiful at maintenance. We save up, pay in advance, and wait for that time of year with the expectation that we are going to be a new man or woman when the conference is over. Don't get me wrong. Conferences aimed to strengthen families or to create an atmosphere to be informed, inspired, and practice spiritual, physical, and emotional healing are priceless. However, these should be the cherry on top rather than the entire pie. In other words, a lack of maintenance creates exhaustion between these short episodes of relief. It is imperative to regularly process, unpack, and release. You do not have to hurry up and wait for relief that's scheduled on a specific date. How much more could you gain from your retreat or conference if you did not spend the entire time unloading offenses, regrets, and resentments?

The Power of Active Listening

James 1:19 says, "My dear brothers and sisters, take note of this: Everyone should be quick to listen, slow to speak and slow to become angry." Does this sound like a superpower rather than a possibility? It is certainly super and powerful, but it is also very possible with intentional daily practice and even more so by the power of the Holy Spirit. When sincere ears are twice as active as the mouth, we double the chances of understanding. Intentionally practicing a "more ear" lifestyle will decrease the likelihood of being offended. Frequently the things that offend us are due to a lack of actively listening with empathy rather than the genuine intent of a person to be offensive.

Active listening is more than just hearing while taking shortcuts to judgments. Instead it fully focuses on the speaker with the intent to understand, comprehend, and respond thoughtfully. Take a moment to process what you heard and do it from the other person's perspective. If possible, calmly repeat back what you heard to the speaker to ensure you received it correctly. Now that you have the correct information with the correct intent, do not rush to respond. This will help in letting "your conversation be always full of grace" (Colossians 4:6). Once you have done this, you can make an informed response as levelheaded as you began. This may seem like it will require a lot of your energy. Actually, you will expend much less energy than the energy required to fuel offenses. And the energy used in active listening and gracious conversation is always energy well spent! When we place our energy in the right place, it will move us peacefully while the pleasant aroma from it blesses all parties. Life may not be as easy as pie, but it can become as fragrant!

When Tuning Out Is Good

Now, at times being full of *it* has nothing at all to do with a person and everything to do with internalizing external trauma. As much as we want to stay informed regarding issues in our country and abroad, allowing too much disturbing news to fill our minds can be traumatizing. It is possible to walk around offended at everyone who looks like the persons who committed crimes of injustice or who publicly supported those crimes. When injustices occur and you have access to live video of brutality, hatred, and inequality, be very careful to know when enough is enough and to simply turn off the television and the computer and take a break from social media. The human mind is not equipped to be bombarded with scenes of ruthless violence and blatant hate. Remain informed, but know when to shut the door and not to reopen it until you have processed the information you have already gained. Power down! Put that stress fire out. You cannot avoid all stress, but some stress you can. Life has enough offenses of its own than to go clicking on more or subscribing to it.

Listen to your body. If after you have taken in news from various media outlets and now your heart and mind are racing, your sleep is affected, your head aches, your muscles become tight, or you're having difficulty with focus, take a step back from it all. Be informed, but not so much that it makes you ill (a unique perspective of ill-informed). There are some things you can fix and others that will come in time. Issues like those mentioned above are the latter. You do not have to drink the entire cistern of news all at once. It is okay to pull away until you know you are ready to reengage. If not, you will become so full of *it* that you may end up being as negative as all the bad news that you have filled yourself with.

That being said, remember to intentionally fill yourself up with good news. Thanks be to Christ our Lord, there is always good news among the dreaded. There is always something to smile about and to be grateful for. There is truth to the saying "a spoonful of sugar helps the medicine go down." You help neutralize emotional trauma related to the barrage of negative media when you refresh yourself regularly with good news. Whether it be time spent in Scripture or googling random acts of kindness as you follow suit, you are filling yourself up with good news and becoming good news too! Remember, you may not be able to immediately change inequality or injustices in this country or world, but you can change one person's life and your own by filling yourself up with, sharing, and being good news.

There are many things in this life that we cannot control, but self-trauma from graphic images and stories is not one of them. One click and a few minutes of your time can lead to a heart full of emotional trauma, restlessness, anxious thoughts, and anger. If you are willing to scroll past opportunities to view graphic images and stories or resist the urge to click, please sign your name after the statement below:

> What I allow to fill my temple is up to me. Disturbing images and stories create an unhealthy atmosphere for my heart and mind. Today, _____/_____/_____ , I make a commitment to refuse to fill up in toxic gas stations with disturbing videos, stories, and graphic images.

> Signed, _____

You have just committed to a plan to improve your mental health. Whether it's mental misery, a bad day, or bad news, you have two choices. You can either do something or not do something. Yes, to not do something is still a choice. A choice was made in Hosea 7:14: "They do not cry out to me from their hearts but wail on their beds. They slash themselves, appealing to their gods for grain and new wine, but they turn away from me." Wailing in their beds, cutting themselves, and reaching out to false hope through false gods was the people's choice. And it was not only a fruitless choice but a self-destructive one. Instead, it is important to create a plan like the one above for when we find ourselves in a fight for our mental health. We can do so much better than wailing, cutting ourselves, and begging for help from impotent sources. We can turn to and rely on God instead.

D.I.A. and M.A.P.

You also need to learn three key words like you know your own name. The three words are "Do It Anyway" (D.I.A.).

You may be in a place mentally where you do not feel like it, but you cannot wait until you are motivated enough to feel like it. Do it anyway.

- Breathe intentionally anyway.
- Worship deeper anyway.
- Process your feelings by journaling anyway.
- Talk it out anyway.
- Go for a walk anyway.
- Even if you must drag yourself, *do it anyway*!

And for those who are in such a dry place that even prayer seems pointless, pray anyway. How? M.A.P. it. What do I mean? If you need to write a prayer out in advance so you can read it on those rough days when you cannot find the words to say, do it. If you know certain seasons, dates, or days of the week are rough for you, M.A.P. (Make A Plan) for those days. While you are in a place that you can find the words, write them, save them, and go to them when you need them.

You can also M.A.P. to pray prepared prayers from your Bible. Jesus prayed David's prayer when he was dying on the cross. David wrote in Psalm 22:1, "My God, my God, why have you forsaken me?" Jesus was in such a condition physically and mentally that he did not try to formulate a new prayer. He prayed what Scripture prayed for him: "My God, my God, why have you forsaken me?" Jesus showed us that we are not alone and that we can even rely on the prayers of those who have gone before us.

There are times we have all been overwhelmed from the inside out or from the outside in. There are times that we all feel forsaken. But remember we are not to remain mentally in a forsaken place. Make sure your plan ends in a praise! Verse 24 of the same psalm exclaims, "For he has not despised or scorned the suffering of the afflicted one; he has not hidden his face from him but has listened to his cry for help." David's troubles would have swallowed him mentally had he not praised God when he did not feel like it. Like David, even when you are full of troubles, offenses, and cares, I encourage you to turn your eyes to heaven and praise God anyway.

Heavenly Father, sometimes there is pain in life that words cannot know. Thank you, Jesus, for being omniscient.

Sometimes there is hurt in life that feels unbearable. Thank you, Jesus, for being a burden bearer.

There are some tears in life that form a river in the soul. Thank you, Jesus, for being a reservoir.

When there is no earthly balm to comfort, I know the One who came "to console those who mourn in Zion, to give them beauty for ashes, the oil of joy for mourning, the garment of praise for the spirit of heaviness" (Isaiah 61:3 NKJV). Thank you, Lord, for showing me the necessity of active and compassionate listening.

Certainly, if you were to punish me for every word or thought that was unkind, I would not be here today. Thank you for helping me become more aware of biases I may hold and helping me to be accountable for them. You told me to love my neighbor as myself, and whenever bias is involved, it contaminates my attempts to do so effectively.

God, I thank you for teaching me to monitor the news I allow to fill me. You have given me enough good news to change me and the entire world. Help me to always remember to go back to that.

Finally, God, help me to intentionally release offenses I have held in my heart. You search the heart and have always known the issues I have tried to hide. I repent now for holding offenses hostage, and I release each one, small and large, to you now.

Thank you for loving me even when I'm full of it and for always loving me well. I love you too. In the name of Jesus, amen.

8

Weight Problem?

Therefore we also, since we are surrounded by
so great a cloud of witnesses, let us lay aside
every weight, and the sin which so easily
ensnares us, and let us run with endurance
the race that is set before us.
—Hebrews 12:1 NKJV

After listing a grand display of faith pioneers in
the eleventh chapter of Hebrews, the apostle Paul
encourages us, "since we are surrounded by so
great a cloud of witnesses, let us lay aside *every weight*,
and *the sin* which so easily ensnares us" (12:1, emphasis
added). Paul is concerned about the weight and the sin.
Out of zealous courtesy, we are often provided with lists

of sometimes biblical and other times man-made dos and don'ts meant to oblige us to recognize sin, but how often are the repercussions of the weight ignored? Yet, until I deal with the weight, I am all the more vulnerable to sin.

The Greek word for "weight" is *ongkos*, which refers to a protuberance or a swelling. It is a noticeable, useless, unhealthy protrusion. It stands out for no good reason as a bulge with no benefits. It does not make one stronger, healthier, or happier, but it certainly makes one heavier. This type of weight has the uncanny ability to appear to be something it is not. The unknowing observer, and even at times the person carrying the weight, may judge this weight to mean a pregnancy. If you have ever made that mistake, you learned quickly not to make an assumption about why someone was carrying extra bodily weight. But the blunder shows that this weight can be an imposter. No, it is not a swelling due to the growing of life within as one may have assumed, but instead it's an uncontrolled and abnormal growth of such proportion that it pulls its victim down—not for the sake of holding life but diminishing it. For instance, I have counseled people who wanted to be free from addiction, but it did not take long to see that the addiction came from the weight of what they went through and things they had done. Once the weight was dealt with, then the addiction could be addressed. The weight must be dealt with before the addiction, eating disorder, promiscuity, or what have you. If there is a weight problem, it is likely the root of other problems.

Throughout this book, we have viewed mental health issues from the outside in through various angles. Now we will deep dive into mental health through a biblical perspective from the inside out. By making personal connections with stories many of us have read and heard as children, we are able to climb onto the counseling couch with our ancient brothers and sisters and learn from the Wonderful Counselor who has always been and will always be concerned about our mental health.

Weight Types

There are at least two types of experiences that become *ongkos* or a weight to us. One is the offense committed against a person that can become a weight *on* a person. The other type is guilt for what a person has done that becomes a weight *in* a person. Two familiar biblical brothers, Jacob and Esau, mirror the truth that you can carry weight as the offender or as the one who was offended.

Jacob and Esau occupied the same womb at the same time. They were twins but vastly different. Because Esau came out of the womb first, he was entitled to the family birthright (Genesis 25:25). The brothers grew up in what would appear to be a healthy environment. Esau and Jacob were raised together in a two-parent home with Isaac and Rebekah as their parents. They were a God-fearing family, and yet they were a dysfunctional family, not unlike many modern-day families.

Whether nondysfunctional or dysfunctional, God welcomes all families to believe on him and receive his grace. I will say that during those times in which my family suffered the most dysfunction were when I appreciated the presence of God in the house of God the most. Whatever state your family may be in, the Bible shows us again and again that you are not the only one; there have been and are other families like yours and mine.

Now, the differences between Esau and Jacob included the different weights they found themselves carrying. One (Esau) carried the weight as the offended, and the other (Jacob) carried the weight as the offender. If both had not dealt with the weight they carried, it would have drained the life out of their living. Their story is a familiar drama many of us first heard in Sunday school. It goes like this. When these brothers reached the appropriate age to receive a blessing from their father, Jacob went to extremely manipulative and deceitful measures to steal Esau's birthright. The familiar children's song about "who stole the cookie from the cookie jar" does not compare to what Esau lost when his birthright was taken. The birthright was a privilege and advantage that the first-born son received among the Jews. The first-born son not only received the greater spiritual blessing of the father, but he also received a double portion of the paternal inheritance along with the authority of the father as the head of the family. When Rebekah, the mother of Jacob and Esau, colluded with Jacob as to how to deceptively obtain Esau's birthright, it was a devastating blow to Esau's familial status and his financial and social future.

The Offender's Weight

Have you ever done something in a selfish or heated moment that seemed like the right thing to do at the time? But when you took time to sit down and actually think about it, you realized the enormity of your error? And so it was with Jacob. His deceit-filled decision affected him. After a good deal of time and maturity, Jacob looked back and painfully observed the trail of hurt from his actions. Allow me to use my imagination of Jacob sitting on the counseling couch. Given the opportunity to process his past, I think he would reveal:

> I never meant to hurt my brother. I coveted what belonged to him and lied to get it, but it was never my intent to hurt him in the process. It's not that I didn't love my brother. When I was afraid, it made me feel better to know that my strong brother was there. He was fearless. We played together in the same fields. I love him. He's my brother. I never meant to hurt him. As a matter of fact, I never even considered that I was hurting him; I was too busy thinking about myself. If anyone had asked me beforehand, I would have said that I would never do something so reprehensible, and I would have meant it!

> I ruined a relationship with the soul I shared
> a womb with and put a wedge where trust
> should've been. In trying to get what I wanted,
> I betrayed my brother.

It's not always that your offender meant to hurt you. It could be that they were so focused on wanting what you had that they never even considered how it would hurt you.

Hindsight is everything. How many times have you heard someone say or even heard the words coming out of your own mouth: "If I knew then what I know now." Of course, if any of us actually knew then what we know now, we would have never misused, taken for granted, manipulated, deceived, furthered that rumor, falsely accused, misrepresented, and the like. The aftermath of our mistakes and premeditated offenses beg for space for us on the counseling couch with Jacob after the damage has been done. Of course, it is *after* the damage has been done that Jacob realizes the enormity of the injuries. Rarely does an offender offend in a vacuum. There's usually some unsuspecting bystander caught in the web of our deceit, mischief, or anger. Jacob's father, Isaac, unknowingly was used to place the nail in the coffin of Esau's future.

I picture Jacob playing the events over in his mind:

> I betrayed not only my twin, but my dying
> father's trust.[2]

Our father, Isaac, was a good man. Dad taught us about God. He told us powerful stories about how God talked with his father, Abraham. He shared his experience on Mount Horeb with us when my grandfather, Abraham, took my dad to sacrifice as a burnt offering at the command of the Lord. He painted a picture of the wood he carried as a young boy walking with his father to sacrifice and his curiosity as to where the sheep was that my grandfather would offer unto God. Our hearts burned as he revealed our grandfather's words, "My son, God will provide for Himself the lamb for a burnt offering."[3] What joy it brings me even now remembering how much our father wanted us to know God as sovereign and as a provider!

Truly, I know my dad loved me, but it was obvious even as a child that he favored Esau more. If I were to be honest, I did too! Esau was always the strong one. I didn't enjoy the danger of hunting, but Esau was skillful at it and my father loved that. It was my brother who made my father's favorite meal. I tried a few times and was excited to bring it to my father, but the reaction was not the same. I had the love of my mother, but I knew who held the heart of my father; it was Esau.[4]

Did that affect me? Of course. It hurt in places that I could not reach to touch. What child does not want to feel as if he has been pleasing in the eyes of his father? But I still would have never imagined that I would go to the lengths I did to betray my father or my brother.

Journal Jewel: Have you ever considered that there may still be a hurting child inside of you in need of healing? What potential does unresolved childhood hurt have on your future actions?

When Jacob stood in front of his blind father with his arms covered in goat skin to look and smell like Esau as he held a meal in his hands that he did not even prepare, it seemed right at the time. And his con worked. He got the birthright that had been rightfully his brother's (Genesis 27:6–29). After accomplishing such a great deception, rather than face the pain of his actions, again at the advice of his mother Jacob ran away from his problem (27:42–28:5). Some years after that, Jacob started his own family, but it did not cure him of the emotional obesity caused by his weight of guilt. It's hard to move on while still carrying the weight of what you did. Jacob could testify that holding on to the weight of your past will yield foolish decisions in your present (29:25).

Decisions while carrying extra weight can cause heavy consequences. Imagine Jacob on the counseling couch responding to the truth of how he moved out but did not truly move on:

> Although I knew what my father-in-law, Laban, was doing to me by giving me Leah instead of Rachel, I felt like I deserved it, so I stayed. I knew he cheated me out of my money,[5] but I felt like I deserved that too, so I stayed. I knew what he was doing when he took advantage of me to make himself richer, but I felt like I deserved that as well, so I stayed. I stayed for twenty years because I felt like I deserved what I was getting. Because I lied, cheated, and betrayed in my past without ever dealing with it, the guilt became a weight, an uncontrollable shame that is controlling my present.

Jacob let guilt reign over twenty years of his life! We romanticize the situation, saying he remained under Laban's thumb because he loved Rachel so much. But Jacob could have taken the same stance to have Rachel much sooner than twenty years. The weight of guilt can hold you hostage as if you are in a maximum security prison when your decisions are for the benefit of your guilt rather than yourself.

Jacob is not alone with his weight issue. If we were to parallel Jacob's situation to our own lives, we would realize that we are not so different. Being filled with the weight of guilt for inflicting hurt produces heavy emotional and relational consequences. Stop and think about what you have done that you realize was hurtful to someone else and set it next to what you are putting up with now. Perhaps someone's thoughts are:

- If I had not had the abortion then, would I attempt to kill every healthy relationship that came my way now?
- If I had not stolen and lied to satisfy my addiction, would I put up with someone else manipulating me years after my sobriety?
- If I had not cheated back then, would I put up with lying and cheating on me now?

Perhaps someone else may admit "He hits me, but the guilt I'm full of keeps telling me I deserve it." The weight says, "Stay and allow him to hit you and then force yourself to believe it when he says he loves you." The weight says, "Stay by his side after he talks to you like a dog, and when he acts like he is leaving, do anything to make him stay." Nobody else in their right mind would continue to punish themselves by living with the same manipulation and deception year after year, but *ongkos* will affect your reasoning.

The guilt we have kept out of courtesy will become our gallows if we do not lay aside the weight by addressing the cause of it. Allowing someone to treat you any kind of way will never soften the guilt, which is why after twenty years Jacob still did not feel any better. You can put yourself through hell and still not feel better. The weight of guilt must be dealt with!

For those who think they can punish themselves for the things they have done, allow me to agitate your reasoning. You cannot pay for the sins you have committed. That's what the cross of Calvary is for! There is no amount of abuse you can do to yourself to make your sins lessen, let alone disappear. You cannot punish yourself enough to make yourself feel better. You cannot sabotage enough relationships that will make your previous wrongs go away. Allowing another person to abuse you will not soften your guilt. That is why after he or she berated you, you still did not feel any better. If you have gone so far as to cut yourself, there is a reason you picked up the blade again—because it did not and will not work. The only way to get better is to deal with the weight.

Not only are self-worth and the expectations for relationships diminished by carrying the weight of guilt, but prayer is affected as well. Prayer requests stay small when guilt stays large. Sometimes our prayer requests are consistently small, not because we are humble and grateful but because we are afraid to trust God's forgiveness and forgetfulness even after our repentance. Meanwhile the Lord lovingly offers himself, saying "I, even I, am he who blots out your transgressions, for my own sake, and remembers your sins no more" (Isaiah 43:25). We make the cross of no effect when we keep taking back the sins that Jesus took care of on the cross. In effect, we say to ourselves, *He took my beating, but I keep beating myself; he took my guilt, but I keep resurrecting it.* Make a conscious choice to lay aside that weight and put it back on the cross where it belongs.

> **Journal Jewel:** Consider the promise of the Lord as mentioned in Isaiah 43:25 in light of Colossians 2:13–14: "You were dead because of your sins and because your sinful nature was not yet cut away. Then God made you alive with Christ, for he forgave all our sins. He canceled the record of the charges against us and took it away by nailing it to the cross." If you struggle with forgiving yourself, write down your guilt next to these two passages. Rx: Read these two scriptures daily as a reminder to let go of the very same things God let go of. If you find yourself tormented by guilt to the degree that it affects your daily life, consider counseling. Set yourself free from the tyranny of guilt.

Yes, you may have been wrong in what you said or did, but holding onto the guilt of that wrong does not make your wrong anymore right. And yet things that come from us, regardless of how wrong, we instinctively attempt to nourish. As abnormal as it is, this type of weight can be difficult to release because it's still something we have produced. When something, rather good or bad, is created from a person's decision and will, that person may have the proclivity to hold on to it, cradle it, and feed it. *It's painful, but I created the pain, so I'll carry it. I created the hurt, so I'll nurse it.* Growth can be healthy, but swelling is always a sign of infection. Holding onto the weight is not what God desires for any of us. It is illegitimate, which is why his Word commands us to lay it aside. God did not father it and his Spirit does not bear witness to it. It's criminal to nurture toxic, abnormal, and uncontrolled hurts, including from long ago, when God says to lay them aside.

Yet regardless of its spiritual illegitimacy, familiarity with even something abnormal can make it difficult to distinguish between healthy weight and overweight, harmless and toxic, spiritual versus carnal. It is possible to carry a weight so long that you no longer recognize its toxicity, heaviness, or perversion. Perhaps a simple test will help you know if what you are carrying is from God or is genuinely a weight problem. If you cannot lift your hands in praise while holding the weight without condemnation, you've got a weight problem. If it came from God, you would not feel condemned by it. The Lord said that he did not come to condemn the world (John 3:17). Paul put it like this: "Therefore, there is now no condemnation for those who are in Christ Jesus" (Romans 8:1). For every offender who is willing to lay aside every weight, the Lord will emancipate you right now. And "if the Son sets you free, you will be free indeed" (John 8:36). You have divine permission—more than that—a divine directive to lay that weight aside.

The beauty in having a friendship with God is that he does not leave us alone even when our actions would push us away from those who love us the most. You can be in Christ and still struggle to deal with your guilt. God was with Jacob after he ran away from his problem at the counsel of his mother. God was still with this offender when he left the home of his father-in-law. While the weight of guilt plagued his soul, God never left Jacob. Yet while blessed with the honorable presence of God, Jacob still had not dealt with his shame. You may walk away from your problems, and God will be with you while you do, but he will not take the guilt you refuse to give to him. The funny thing about trying to run away is that wherever you end up, you are still stuck with the you that you never dealt with. Eventually, you will have to deal with the weight on you.

> **Journal Jewel:** We can all relate to Jacob on some level. Write and reflect on your experiences as the offender, and honestly discover if you are still holding on to any of the weight it has caused or may still be causing in your life.

The Offended's Weight

Let's turn for a moment to the other brother, Esau, sitting on the couch. As much as some people may relate to

Jacob, others suffer the weight that Esau carried. Perhaps you were the unsuspecting trusting soul that someone else took advantage of. Recall that Esau was not the offender but the offended. Imagine his dismay when he entered his father's house in anticipation to receive what was promised to him only to realize the double betrayal! Not only did his brother betray him, but his mother helped Jacob carry out his deception. With tears he must have cried "Jacob! My brother! How could you! I trusted you! I loved you! How could you do what you did to me? And my mother who nursed me, raised, and cared for me, how could you? I always knew you favored Jacob over me, but how could you go this far?"[6]

You may not have had your birthright stolen, but someone may have stolen your heart by means of deception. Like Jacob, they were not who they presented themselves to be. They covered up so well that you were completely taken off guard when their love language slowly turned to verbal abuse, when their tender caresses gradually materialized into a grip and a clenched fist. They stole your innocence and abused it. Now some time has passed and your Jacob (deceiver) has moved on, but perhaps some weight was gained from the past that you've not yet laid aside. Rather than seeking healing when they left, you've cradled it as if it were your own. Once again, I hear God saying, *Why are you cradling something that is lacking my spiritual DNA? Why are you nursing what was not meant to be bred by you?*

Are you trying to move forward, but with a heavy weight? Wanting to get on with your life but emotionally holding on to illegitimate affliction? The proverbial Jacob moved out of the city, but are you still here holding the pain of what he did? Could it be that he or she packed up all their belongings, but you held onto the only thing that you could when they left—unforgiveness? The weight of unforgiveness can become as normal as your pillow, coffee, and dinner. It can become the commonality of the day to remember what they did to you, and then you start to boil within.

Perhaps you dealt with this by switching jobs. But no matter the career change, you still can't find any satisfaction. It's hard to be content and heavy at the same time.

Maybe you moved to a new city, but the emotional breakdowns moved in with you because it is impossible to be at peace and heavy at the same time.

You may have developed some new relationships, but these aren't helping either. New relationships come and go, but the only constant in the bedroom of your heart is the unforgiveness that has become a trusted pillow.

Journal Jewel: We can all relate to Esau on some level. Write and reflect on your experiences as the offended and honestly discover if you are still holding on to any of the weight it has caused or may still be causing in your life.

You may be thinking, *But that is not even half of the story!* It was not for Esau either. When someone you trust betrays you, it's hard not to look at other loved ones as being complicit in the crime even if they weren't. In addition to the purposeful betrayal of his mother and brother, Esau had to consider his father's role in the drama. I can hear Esau on the counseling couch now: "Daddy! How could you not recognize me? You should have known me! I thought I was special to you!" Offenses from a parent are perhaps the most difficult to conceive because it goes against the very nature of their role. I believe Esau looked at Isaac and said something like this to him or within himself: "Daddy, yes Jacob posed as an imposter, but you out of all people, dad you should've known me! Daddy, I thought you favored me. I don't care what Jacob was covered up with. How could you not know me?"

Fathers who do not acknowledge and perhaps could not even recognize their children are all too common. When our natural fathers will not recognize or acknowledge our presence, it creates a distrust in our hearts for our heavenly Father. Because we often relate our experiences with our earthly fathers as the template of expectation for our heavenly Father, it is important to note that God is not like Isaac. God knows what and who is his.

Likewise, God is also not fooled by our dancing and singing over our weight. Praise will never cover up our weight! It's futile to praise God and blame him at the same time. Some people refuse to fully give themselves to ministry they are called to because they secretly blame God for their weight. Even when the abnormal growth in the heart beats along with the heart as if everything is normal, the Lord searches our heart and examines our mind (Jeremiah 17:10).

God never sits idly by. He is always working; he never slumbers or sleeps. Like a good Father, the Lord is fully invested in the lives of his children. I hear the Wonderful Counselor proclaim:

> I am not Isaac. I know what came from me.[7] I will never be fooled by the hair of a goat. I know every single hair that is on your head. I've numbered them.[8] I am God and cannot be fooled.
>
> Stop blaming, rejecting, and ignoring me because of Isaac's mistakes. I love you! I loved you then, and I love you now! Look to me, the author and finisher of your faith. For the joy that was set before me, I endured the cross.[9] I disregarded the shame, the offense, the transgression inflicted upon and against me because I knew the joy that was before me.
>
> Follow my lead. I carried the cross for you as long as I had to, but I did not carry it forever. I carried the offense for as long as I had to, but I did not carry it forever. I carried the pain for as long as I had to, but I did not carry it forever. I carried the insults, the false accusations, the

hecklers, but I did not carry them forever. I carried the weight of the cross as long as I had to, and I did not go back to pick up the cross after I rose from the dead. When I ascended into heaven, the cross remained on earth. I laid that weight down, but my joy is forever.

You must let go of the weight because joy still awaits you.

Journal Jewel: Have you felt a sense of false comfort or control by holding onto the weight of unforgiveness? If you chose to forgive and place that perceived control in the hands of our Wonderful Counselor, what comfort could he provide? Here are some biblical passages to consider: Psalm 34:10; Proverbs 3:5–6; John 10:10; 14:27; 2 Corinthians 9:8.

The Way to Weight Loss

Jacob and Esau, the offender and the offended, would eventually be given a divine opportunity to lay aside their weight for the sake of joy and peace. Although it would have perhaps been nice if they could have planned ahead as to when, where, and how it would happen, they would both have to face the past and one another.

We think it ideal to come to grips with our weight on our own terms. However, the same God that has never left throughout the entirety of the saga is the same God who will orchestrate opportunities for reconciliation. God loves reconciliation! It is why he gave his only begotten Son!

Ironically, God sends Jacob right back to the place where he perpetrated his crimes. "Then the LORD said to Jacob, 'Return to the land of your father and grandfather and to your relatives there, and I will be with you'" (Genesis 31:3 NLT). In due time, God sent Jacob back to once and for all lay aside the weight. This was no easy task. Jacob was terrified when he heard that Esau was coming his way (32:7). Facing those we have wronged is necessary, but not necessarily easy. Out of fear, Jacob placed his wife Leah in one group and his wife Rachel in another group. He thought to himself, "If Esau meets one group and attacks it, perhaps the other group can escape" (v. 8). He was afraid and preparing for casualties.

Journal Jewel: What fears are hindering you from facing those individuals you have wronged so you can strive for reconciliation? Have you shared those fears with the Wonderful Counselor through prayer? If not, why?

We can all relate to Jacob's fear, but it's his response to fear that saves his life. In the face of fear, he began to pray. He told God that he was afraid for his family (v. 11). There's something about opening your mouth and telling God where it hurts.

- "God, I'm afraid that my marriage is failing."
- "Lord, I'm afraid that my child is out of control, and I don't know what else I can do to help."
- "I'm afraid, Father, that my finances aren't enough to meet my needs."
- "God, I'm afraid!"

For every silent scream you cried, God leaned in, bent his ear, and responded. For every unutterable heartache you wept, God is sustaining and refreshing you. For each sigh of exasperation, God is sending his spirit to renew and comfort. For every dark and dreary moment, God sends warming light. For every inner groan of *I'm not okay*, the Lord says, *I know, and I'm here.*

Telling the Lord your fears is good, but you can't stop there. You have to finish like Jacob did. After Jacob confessed his fears, he began to proclaim the promises God spoke over his life. He announces his fears, but then announces his faith, saying, "But you promised me, 'I will surely treat you kindly, and I will multiply your descendants until they become as numerous as the sands along the seashore—too many to count'" (v. 12 NLT).

If you are to be comfortable with telling God your fears, surely you ought to be confident in telling God his Word. When you are afraid because of lack, remind God:

- Lord, you said to "Give, and it will be given to you. A good measure, pressed down, shaken together and running over, will be poured into your lap. For with the measure you use, it will be measured to you" (Luke 6:38).

- God, I'm overwhelmed with the fear of being a single parent, but you are the Lord who "gives strength to the weary and increases the power of the weak" (Isaiah 40:29).

- When I'm afraid that I might lose my mind, Lord, your Word promises "the peace of God, which transcends all understanding, will guard your hearts and your minds in Christ Jesus" (Philippians 4:7).

And when the enemy has the audacity to discourage you that prayer doesn't work, remind God of what he said: "Before they call I will answer; while they are still speaking I will hear" (Isaiah 65:24). Our progress is tied up in our prayer!

Jacob was alone that night until the angel of God showed up. Through prayer, Jacob gained the strength to wrestle with the angel to the break of day (Genesis 32:24). I believe this was a time of Jacob wrestling with the weight of his guilt as well and finally determining to lay it aside and live in his present. After wrestling with himself and the angel, the angel announced, "Your name shall no longer be called Jacob, but Israel; for you have struggled with God and with men, and have prevailed" (v. 28 NKJV). You struggled with the weight. You struggled with the guilt. You then humbled yourself and faced your guilt and prevailed.

This was Jacob's preparation for the meeting with Esau that he had been so very anxious about.

> **Journal Jewel:** Have you ever become so comfortable with the weight of unforgiveness or guilt that you settled to simply live with it? How differently would the account of Jacob and Esau have turned out had they done the same? How differently would your present and future be if you chose to lay aside the weight?

After all that Jacob had done to scheme and connive against his brother, perhaps we would expect that when Esau saw him that he would still see a deceiver and a liar, as the name Jacob implies. But Esau had taken the time to heal and lose some weight as well. "Esau ran to meet Jacob and embraced him; he threw his arms around his neck and kissed him. And they wept" (33:4). What could have been a Jerry Springer episode of tirades and accusations became an encounter of reconciliation, forgiveness, and love.

Come on Jacob.

Come on Esau.

Come on offender.

Come on offended.

God wants to minister to both. Not Jacob or anyone of us caught God by surprise when we fell short or fell long. God had the remedy for all of us before we offended.

As soon as Adam and Eve fell, God gave the cure (Genesis 3:15). The cure is here and has been for a long time. His name is Jesus.

Your name may not have been Jacob or Esau. Regardless, you are more than what you experienced, and you do not have to be what you have done.

Journal Jewel: If you could imagine sitting on the counseling couch with Jacob and Esau, which part of their conversation would you most connect to and why?

Your name may have been unforgiveness, bitterness, deceiver, resentment, shame, guilt, or condemnation, but if you would right now humble yourself, repent, and forgive, you will become Israel. Lay aside the weight you are dying to hold on to and embrace the love of Christ. You do not have to pray afraid that God is mad at you. You do not have to attempt to punish yourself or allow anyone else to punish you. You can praise him without being ashamed.

When I learned for myself that I cannot make Living Water dirty and that Living Water can make the murkiest water clean, I freely surrendered my weight and sin. I implore you to step right in. The water is good, healing, and freeing. There are many of us who freely wade in that cleansing water right now. Join us.

Dear Father, I thank you for every wound you received for my transgressions. As terrible as it sounds, there are no bruises as powerful and beautiful as those you received for my iniquities. After enduring such a sacrifice, you see me broken-hearted and sorrowful in spirit, and you still decree "I will give you a new heart and put a new spirit in you" (Ezekiel 36:26). Just when I started to believe the degrading names I was called, you gave me a new name.

I am grateful for the transparency of your Word that shows me, I am not the only one who has suffered nor am I the only one who has caused suffering. But you, oh Lord, are the only One who can heal the suffering and deliver the transgressor. In your sovereign hands, I lay this weight—this unsightly hindrance that has held me hostage. I held onto it thinking I deserved it or that the offender deserved my unforgiveness, but I was wrong. I am determined to run this race with freedom, joy, and peace, and by your grace I will do just that. Oh, and Father, I love you too.

9

A Healthy Immune System

But Jesus knew their thoughts, and said to them:
"Every kingdom divided against itself is brought
to desolation, and every city or house divided
against itself will not stand."
—Matthew 12:25 NKJV

What if we were more intentional about the relationships we formed? The human life of Jesus reveals that there may be many with whom you interact (Matthew 5:1; 7:28; 9:8; 12:23; 13:2), few with whom you closely connect (Matthew 10:1–4), and even fewer you invite into the most intense and intimate moments of your life (Matthew 26:36–38). Although crowds followed Jesus, those crowds were not a representation of friendship.

In fact, John 6:2 alludes to the fact that some of the crowds were there solely for the excitement and expectation of miracles. A hard pill to swallow is that there may be some in our lives who are there only to receive from us or to be entertained. And yet, we can find solace in knowing that once the crowd leaves (and they will), there are those who will remain close to us. And greater peace in understanding true intimacy is likely found in the very few. Yes, it is wisdom to know that not everyone is a friend regardless of their proximity or professions. Being a Christian does not mean that we are to embrace everyone as a friend. The life of Jesus reveals the importance of carefully choosing who you allow into the personal spaces of your life.

We cannot be so afraid of having less relationships that we will allow a monster to attach to us as long as we can call it a friend. I have counseled young and older people who were dying to hold on to toxic relationships. They kept waiting for some sign in the form of a writing on the wall, a dramatic shout from heaven, or some sign in the sky, not realizing that they were already showing signs of toxicity: confusion, anxiety, low self-concept, emotional trauma, withdrawal from loved ones, fear, and depression. When signs of toxic behavior are recognized after the relationship is formed, many have felt they are now too invested to part ways. As if in an effort to become a sacrificial lamb, they allowed others to find peace at the expense of their sanity. It seemed the toxic people in their lives could only be at peace if others were at their wits end.

In order to disinfect from the unhealthy, there would first have to be a disconnect.

Getting Healthy and Its Benefits

Healthy relationships are born from intentional self-respect, mutual respect, consideration of others, active listening, and communication fostered with honest emotional availability and time. When these characteristics are truly in place, you are less likely to miss red flags that may be signs of a virus growing rather than a relationship developing. Perhaps you have personal experience, or you witnessed others catch relationships like a person with a poor immune system catches a cold. The relationship lasts for a short time and the person finally gets over it until the next cold. The cold is so "common" that it never occurs to the person to build their immune system. At this rate, it's inevitable to end up catching more than just what's become common. They move from relationship to relationship catching feelings, catching trauma, and perhaps even catching disease, never realizing they have dropped important things as they hold on to viruses they caught and become susceptible to catching others.

As obvious as the symptoms of a cold may be, the virus itself is undetectable to the eye, even as it begins to replicate itself. And yet as it multiplies, so does the misery it causes. In an unhealthy relationship, one will begin to see an increase in symptoms or virus-related behaviors, such as:

- jealousy
- manipulation
- being controlling or overbearing
- unable to consider another's point of view
- having to always be right
- being emotionally unavailable
- projecting their shortcomings onto others
- unable to show empathy
- casting blame or faults for their own wrongs

These behaviors likely did not show all at once. Gradually they replicate until the person begins to bear the miserable symptoms of infection. In turn, the host may learn to walk on eggshells to lessen the misery.

Regardless of the rate of infection, one does not have to keep it in one's life. Jesus Christ died not only to free us from the entanglements of sin, but he came that we might have life and that more abundantly. If at any time we find ourselves headed back toward the lifeless corruption and deprivation he freed us from, we should remind ourselves of the enormous urgency and gravity of the price he paid to free us. His life and death free us, not anyone else's. This means the decision to stay in a toxic relationship for the purpose of changing the other person is futile. You are not the Lord, and neither am I. We cannot save anyone, though he can. Many people have broken themselves while trying to fix someone else. You cannot save a person from being who they are, but you can liberate yourself from further sickness, fatigue, confusion, and degradation by getting out. Regardless of the length of time you put in, do not count the time invested in the relationship as a loss but as invaluable lessons learned. The lessons may have been hard ones, but you gained critical knowledge to add to your mental health toolbox and to facilitate healthier relationships in the future.

Thankfully, you do not have to give past experiences the power to determine your future. If you cannot take anything else positive away from an experience, take this: any experience is just that, an experience which means knowledge gained through exposure. You've gained knowledge of what works or what does not work, which is more than you knew before. Regardless of the experience, you can and should expect to love and be loved in a healthy and whole manner.

Indie Arie sings a song titled "I Am Ready for Love." The title implies preparation, and I believe that preparedness is a necessity. My husband has a motto: "If you feel like you deserve something, then make sure you are ready for it when it happens." Purposefully looking within before looking without creates a win-win situation. There is an intentionality that exists when healthy relationships are developed. No one catches healthy relationships. It is not by mistake, unlike catching a cold. Prior to considering a relationship, it is imperative to build up the immune system: your self-love, self-worth, self-knowledge, and a God-inspired vision for your life. These attributes are not only personal blessings but blessings to all those with whom we form relationships. Before we can ever obey one of the greatest commandments, to love our neighbor as ourselves (Mark 12:31), we must first actually love ourselves.

A healthy immune system will assist in discerning whether a relationship should be formed in the first place. In taking the necessary time to ready ourselves for caring connections, we must remain cognizant that previous painful relationships are not a mirror of all relationships. However, if past relationships are our only archetype, we may feel hopeless. Whoever suggested the expression "Good people are hard to come by" had a rearview mirror but was lacking a front window.

Enjoy the journey and take your time. The impulsivity of rushing into a relationship steals the opportunity of time, which stunts the growth of healthy relationships and increases the likelihood of viruses. Impulsivity is the death of growth. Refuse the temptation to satisfy the now at the expense of a healthier future. Rash decisions can be likened to just that, a rash. You have to scratch the itch regardless of how much worse it will make your condition. You have to respond (scratch it) now. You have to say yes (scratch it) now. Instead, take your time. With time, opportunities will come for the person you are engaging with to become angry, disappointed, tempted, or frustrated. You want to observe how that person responds in varying situations. There is more information (good or not-so-good) given during raw situations than there is communicated during preplanned dates. With time, you will observe if the advertised integrity, kindness, and honesty are generally true or disingenuous.

Had we only understood the practicality and value of entering into relationships responsibly, we would save ourselves and others from emotional carnage. If I were to ask everyone reading this book to raise their hand if their relationships, past or present, have ever negatively affected their mental health, everyone would raise their hands. Yet research has shown that healthy relationships lead to longer life spans and even foster physical healing by strengthening the immune system.[10] If this is the case, the longer we entertain unhealthy relationships, the lesser the quality and quantity of our years. And yet, it is fully possible to redeem the time and intentionally foster healthier relationships in your life.

Walled-In: An Unhealthy Alternative

A healthy immune system (self-love, self-worth, self-knowledge, and a God-inspired vision for your life) is best practice for relationships, mental health, growth, and abundant living. However, no one ever said it was the easiest practice. If you are like me, you may have tried other, more simple options. Instead of doing all that self-work stuff to instead do something more permanent and less invasive. Yes, I once chose to put up walls instead of building a healthy immune system. It seemed like a good plan at the time. I did not have to look within to learn to love me or consider my worth or who I was. I did not have to bother with considering the will of God for my life. I did not have to forgive myself or others. I also would not hate or retaliate. I would not perseverate on the perceived wrong. Instead, I determined I would erect walls to protect me from ever being vulnerable to others again.

Over time, I found that the walls had done their job, but the side effects were unsightly. I created walls, separating me from others, preventing me from getting close enough to be bitten again. However, it also prevented me from getting close enough to be held or to sincerely comfort others. To free myself from the prison I built, I would have to painstakingly deconstruct the walls I assembled and then go about the work of rebuilding my immune system.

> **Journal Jewel:** What are some of the obstacles you face in even considering adopting self-love, self-worth, and self-knowledge? What will you do to overcome these obstacles?

Years later, I visited the tranquil and well-manicured Lexington Cemetery which was a stark reminder of the consequences of choosing to wall myself in. I was born and raised in Lexington, Kentucky, but had no idea that another cemetery was juxtaposed to the one I now stood in. I never knew that this other cemetery was there because a wall separated the two, and the wall was completely covered over with vines. When the wall was pointed out behind the manicured vines and flowers, I could only imagine it was there to support such a unique sense of beauty. It was not until I made the journey to the other side of the wall that its true purpose became glaringly visible. The wall was created during segregation to separate the graves of white people from the graves of black people. Although desegregation has since occurred, the wall continues to do its job, creating a palpable and shocking difference between the two cemeteries. The level of upkeep and beautification on one side of the wall was in mint condition, whereas the other side was grown over and unkempt. If that wall were to come down, creating an opening for visitors to see both cemeteries, there would be an urgency to ensure both spaces bore the same semblance of serene beauty. The wall was erected during a time of division and inequity, and it still preserved some of the results of that historical time.

The purpose of that one wall was like the many I had built. I wanted to keep out what I feared and protect myself from preconceived ideas. For me, these were ideas concerning pain and relationships. The wall served its purpose. It kept the unwanted out, but in doing so, it made me two-faced. One side of me, the one I did not mind "the right" people seeing, was well kept and nurtured, while the other side of me was overrun, cold, neglected, and certainly a place unsuitable for rest or peace. The irony is, just like that cemetery, I was not truly living. I was too busy guarding, constructing, and patrolling to enjoy living. I experienced a sobering truth: a "house divided against itself will not stand" (Matthew 12:25 NKJV).

Jabez prayed for God to enlarge his territory (1 Chronicles 4:10). I asked God for the same during the same season I walled myself in, but the walls made it impossible to step into what I asked God to enlarge. Walls hinder the entering in of the very blessings that we pray for. Even if God were to enlarge the territory, the walls hinder the experience of being able to walk into the blessing. Once I recognized the walls had to come down, I realized that the job was too big for me. Although I had constructed the walls, they now seemed impregnable, much like the walls of Jericho must have seemed to the Hebrew people (Joshua 6).

Some people have been building walls since childhood due to their experience of abuse or neglect. They have years of brick and mortar to undue. Periods of reinforcements from bad relationships and toxic connections add more brick and mortar. The walls may be strengthened by sharp words from those who said they loved us, what the enemy whispered into our ears, and what past failures echo. Still, the more we live inside of those walls, the more comfortable we can become with the one-sided scenery. After all, we know what's *inside* the walls; we know how to function there. It's what is *outside* of the walls that may challenge us and even cause us fear. What will we find there? Even if we're lonely inside, the known loneliness may be more pacifying than the unknown outside. We may say to ourselves, *I see what is in here, and although what I see has to be emotionally and spiritually unhealthy, because I have seen it long enough, I have come to accept it and learn to appreciate it.*

"For we live by faith, not by sight" (2 Corinthians 5:7) was more of a cliché for me as a master wall builder. And as a believer, it is hard to accept that the very walls assembled to prevent hurt have instead hardened the heart. It may be sobering to admit you cannot get out, and no one else can get in. Boundaries are essential. But by all means avoid building walls that prevent progress. If you are to grow, love, and live, your walls must come down, and your immune system must be rebuilt.

> **Journal Jewel:** Was there a time in your life you decided to build walls? How long have your walls been standing? What have the walls prevented you from doing or experiencing in your life?

Bringing Down the Walls

In the historical and epic account of the divine demolition found in Joshua 6, Israel had many options of other cities in Canaan that they could have conquered first. Instead, the Lord commanded they start with Jericho, the strongest and the most fortified city in all of the land. Jericho had walls twenty-five feet high and twenty feet thick. Having looked at the intimidating walls, surely someone had to have pointed out some smaller ones to start with instead. "God, can we maybe consider a territory where the walls are not so massive?" The walls of Jericho would have remained standing if Israel moved alone in her own strength.

Often the reason we attempt to take down smaller obstructions in our lives is because we prepare to overcome in our own strength. You may have been preparing to handle this issue you built on your own—with your own intellect, will, and wit—but walls this strong need more power to be taken down. Perhaps you've suffered great pain and have erected high, thick, Jericho-type walls as a result. Your pain managed the building of the walls, and only healing and forgiveness by the help of God will bring them down.

> **Journal Jewel:** How would your Joshua chapter 6 experience read? Would it say, "I huffed and I puffed and tried to blow the house down"? Or "I took down a few bricks and then quickly put them back in when someone got close"? Would it read, "I painted the wall to make it look pleasant, and I'm still looking at the wall"? If your walls are still standing, how's your life story playing out? Is it really any better? What are some ways you can begin to truly deconstruct the walls you built?

With the help of God, your walls will begin to give way as you actively forgive others as well as yourself for any supporting role you may have played in the saga. Acknowledge the feelings attached to both forgiving yourself and others. However, do not allow your feelings to override your faith in the healing power of God. Continue forgiving, and you will continue healing. The walls will come down in alignment with this process, and you will begin to enjoy the freedom to grow, to love, and to be loved. "If the Son sets you free, you will be free indeed" (John 8:36). True freedom is being able to look your enemy in the eye without malice in your heart. Regardless of how long and strong your walls stood, freedom is having a past without your past having you. Live in the freedom of God's generous grace. These measures will not ensure you are never hurt again, but they will ensure your immune system is healthy enough to endure and even thrive in spite of it.

Also understand that you should not wait to feel forgiveness of yourself and others before you receive the fruit of the act of forgiveness. You may immediately want to "feel" the weight of unforgiveness lifted or "feel" the walls come down, but the genuine evidence of forgiveness will be in your ability to operate beyond the walls that once stood. Feelings are fleeting. Therefore, they cannot be a measuring stick for progress and certainly not for faith. For instance, just because one does not feel in love does not mean one is not married. Just because one does not feel goosebumps every time the Bible is opened does not mean one is not saved by grace. Marriage is not a feeling; it is a fact. Faith is not a feeling; it is fully believing that Jesus Christ died and rose from the grave (Romans 10:9). We do not always walk around feeling a warm glow because of our salvation, but we walk in the fact of our faith and not the flimsiness of our feelings.

We do not pray for a feeling for feelings are never permanent. We pray for the results of our faith in the power of God to manifest. You will not always feel forgiven; but when you confess your sins, you receive his forgiveness based on the fact of your faith in his Word (1 John 1:9). When you forgive others, you may not immediately "feel it," but it will manifest first in you and then around you as the walls begin to fall. Do not allow a feeling or its absence to throw you off course. Because you are emotional does not mean God is in it. Because you are not emotional does not mean God isn't involved and working. Feelings do not validate or invalidate facts.

As you begin to see evidence of the walls falling and prepare for fresh connections, determine your inner circle from your developing healthy immune system—that place of self-love, self-worth, self-knowledge, and a God-inspired vision for your life. Remember, a healthy immune system will assist in discerning whether a relationship should be formed in the first place. Oh yes, walls were built because some individuals who drew near you to greet you with "hell*o*" only placed the "o" there as a disguise. Their true introduction and intentions were "hell." It was only after having your trust and goods devastated that the finances, sweat, and energy once invested into relationships were then fully thrust into erecting walls. Now that the walls have or are coming down, you can use that powerful energy and those resources for intentional healthy relationships.

When your walls are finally coming down or have completely toppled over, you will find a wonderful and literal opening of opportunity. The purpose of the opportunity is not to find a partner, spouse, or friend, but simply to engage conscientiously with another human being. If you truly engage with a healthy immune system, you will promote healthy conversations and engagement, which lead to intentional and healthier relationships. Remember, whether you're dealing with relationships or wrecking hurtful walls, God desires to be the author and the finisher. As you learn to love yourself and others through God, you must ask him to bless your introspection, discernment, and intentionality to yield healthy and whole relationships. Now invite God in.

Father, I thank you for protecting me from myself. I have made choices out of despair, impulsivity, poor self-concept, and perhaps from poor or nonexistent examples in my childhood. As difficult as the consequences of toxic relationships have been, it could have been worse, costing my very life. You have been merciful and gracious, allowing me to make my own decisions and yet not leaving me when what I chose again and again ended in painful disgrace. Each time, you pick me up, hold me close, and show me a better way through your

Word. I have not always wanted to hear the truth. But you continually give it to me with love.

Lord, many times I have easily judged (mostly misjudged) others, and I have been divided: disgruntled while appearing delighted, broken while attempting to blend, hurting with a facade of happiness. I know it is your desire that I be whole.

The walls in my life are as intimidating and formidable as the walls of Jericho. It is not possible to bring them down in my own strength. But your grace is sufficient for me, for your power is made perfect in weakness (2 Corinthians 12:9). I yield to the working of your Holy Spirit and seek to sincerely cooperate with your will.

Lord, I forgive those who hurt and misused me. I ask that you bring healing there. I forgive myself for building a prison and intentionally shutting others out. I ask that you bring healing there. As forgiveness and healing reach within and out, I ask that you would break down these walls imprisoning me and keeping me from loving, growing, and giving. Demolish each wall hindering me from receiving the love of others. Thank you in advance for fresh friendships and the renewal of relationships on the other side of the wall.

I am eternally grateful that you never put a wall up so that I could no longer get to you in spite of how I treated you. Instead, you ensured the par-

tition would be ripped in two forever because you were determined for me to have full access to you.

As I now submit to your love, I ask for you to bless my endeavors toward healthy and whole relationships. Bless those who will be a part of my life with wisdom and health. Enable me to be able to be a blessing to those whom I will form relationships. I thank you in advance for every healthy and whole relationship to come. You are the epitome of love, and my heart's desire is to follow your example. In your precious name, Jesus, I pray. Amen.

10

Empowering Empathy

For we do not have a high priest who is unable to empathize
with our weaknesses, but we have one who has been
tempted in every way, just as we are—yet he did not sin.
—Hebrews 4:15

The human heart endures brokenness, yet in resilience, desperately reaches for love again. Though its doors unknowingly welcome thieves, given time the heart renews trust to open yet again. Though its windows shatter defiled by intruders, somehow the longing for sunshine rejects the permanency of bars and shades. Made in his image, within us is a desire, a longing to love and to be loved. Our Creator *is* love, and so our hearts beat on. When you find yourself angry that you actually care after trying to convince yourself you do not, don't be dismayed. Rather, smile and thank God that you are your Father's child.

You may have experienced the failed trial of attempting not to care for someone, trying to make up your mind that you never really loved the person who left. Then reality strikes and you realize you still do genuinely care for them. You may kick yourself every time you realize you were so hurt knowing that in order to truly be hurt by someone, you have to truly care for someone. May I put your mind at ease? Jesus loved Judas, the disciple who eventually betrayed him. Jesus loved his accusers, and the Roman guards who beat and crucified him. Jesus also loves you and me, all the while knowing that we have sometimes been bitter and resentful toward him and have made countless mistakes and committed intentional outright wrongs. To continue to care for our detractors, gossipers, and slanderers is a trait we gained from our Father.

Any energy placed into trying to hold on to anger or vengeance would be better served by speaking in agreement with the Spirit who lives in us, "Father, forgive them, for they know not what they do" (Luke 23:34 NKJV). Pray it until your heart fully agrees, releasing you from the torment of unforgiveness. Pride would call that foolish. Your very real pain would call that reckless. Our Father, however, calls it love.

Journal Jewel: Have you ever felt shame for loving someone who did not appreciate your love? I'm not referring to allowing oneself to be abused by another. I'm referring to genuine love that yet prays for its accusers, sincerely wishes salvation for its detractors, and passionately desires that its enemy be made whole. Whether the shame for continuing to love came from within or from without, throw away the shame and embrace the reflection of your Father that you see in the mirror and in your actions. Luke 6:31–36 from The Message explains this truth with clarity:

> Here is a simple rule of thumb for behavior: Ask yourself what you want people to do for you; then grab the initiative and do it for *them*! If you only love the lovable, do you expect a pat on the back? Run-of-the-mill sinners do that. If you only help those who help you, do you expect a medal? Garden-variety sinners do that. If you only give for what you hope to get out of it, do you think that's charity? The stingiest of pawnbrokers does that.
>
> I tell you, love your enemies. Help and give without expecting a return. You'll never—I promise—regret it. Live out this God-created identity the way our Father lives toward us, generously and graciously, even when we're at our worst. Our Father is kind; you be kind.

Love Is . . .

Love is not indifferent. It feels and cares deeply.

Love does not have an expiration date. Its aroma is enjoyed even in the worst of storms and earthquakes throughout a lifetime.

Love cannot be bought. It remains faithfully invested when the market rises and falls.

When love is not reciprocated, it is common to internalize why not, especially if there has been a recurring theme of betrayal, abandonment, or neglect in your life. Because "as he thinks in his heart, so is he" (Proverbs 23:7 NKJV), internalizing falsehoods of low self-worth, incompetence, or undesirableness can make the heart and mind resemble a graveyard teeming with death and decay. But you need to understand that how another person treated you is never an indication of your worth or status. The truth is, you are worthwhile with limitless possibilities. You are loved to the cross, to an empty tomb, and into eternity. You are a masterpiece ordained not just to be here but to be present. You are "so loved" (John 3:16 NKJV), and there is absolutely nothing you nor anyone else can do to take that away. There is no sin that could be committed against you to change these truths nor failure you could succumb to that would lessen them.

I am grateful to have experienced what love is, especially the love of Christ, the love of family, and the love of friends. We used to sing a song when I was a child that said "Count your blessings, name them one by one."[11]

Thankfully, I held that song close into adulthood, into life's storms and through painful situations. It's imperative to remain intentionally appreciative for the love you receive, and you will be less disappointed for the love you do not. Yes, we need to be appreciative and grateful no matter what we go through. We need to count our blessings. To take for granted precious and timeless gifts is like keeping your lamp under your bed; the light remains, but the effectiveness is utterly lost, leaving you to stumble about needlessly. Regardless of the pain imposed by betrayal or rejection, it does not lessen the brightness of the lamp you already have. Place it where you can see it, be inspired by it, and see others better because of it. As you're counting blessings, there are times you may still have to deal with the pain of brokenheartedness, but by all means don't stop counting while you're dealing.

Journal Jewel: Take a few moments to give thanks for each blessing in your life and write down as many as you can (i.e., salvation, life, health, strength, food, gifts, talents, testimonies, transportation, friendships, employment, your pastor, your church family, pets, a sunny or snowy day, refreshing rain, the sound of the birds, the smells and sights of autumn or spring, and so on).

Another's Shoes

I once met a young man who entered the lives of others well liked and exited their lives well disliked. Because he was hilarious and outgoing, he initially won their attention and friendship. His humor was infectious and could cause an entire room to laugh aloud. Very soon, however, those newfound friends would find themselves out of money he claimed to borrow. He would then disappear into thin air, a recurring magic trick he became well known for.

Anger may have been the natural reaction people had to this individual's behavior. However, upon processing him and his actions, empathy would be the healthiest emotional response. This young man was raised with deception and manipulation as the standard, and honesty and communication as the last resort. His mother passed away when he was young, and his father constantly and blatantly lied, broke promises, manipulated, and stole. This was life's curriculum that this young man received through his early years and into adulthood. It was his foundation. He truly had no idea how to continue in a relationship with honesty and trust.

This was not a young man who needed someone to hold judgment against him but empathy for him. He may not change anytime soon, but hatred, resentment, or anger would not help him or those impacted by his actions. He had already taken enough from his "friends"; to give him their peace as well would not be wise. Likewise, he had enough taken from him already; to take their love away would be cruel and unusual punishment.

On the other hand, the decision to show compassion with those who hurt us blesses the hurt and the hurting. This ability is born from our heavenly Father and nurtured through our learning to empathize with others. Empathy steps into the shoes even of those who have wronged us in order to understand their perspective and feelings. Empathy then uses that information to respond thoughtfully and compassionately. Might I add, the shoes in the case of the young man were lonely, scattered, and broken. When I imagined walking in them, it caused me back pain and heartache. Fresh hope is possible for both him and those who make the decision to empathize rather than criticize. Seeing the person who has committed harmful behaviors in this way helps us see that they, too, are sinful, hurting, and imperfect as we are.

Let's take a moment to try an exercise in empathy. After taking a few deep cleansing breaths, consider why a sensible person would do something like this and how they may have felt. It can be difficult to even consider, but in setting yourself to understand others, you gain a better understanding of yourself as well. From that place of empathy, you free yourself from entanglements of wrath, bitterness, and hate. Empathy helps us see and relate to humanity in the midst of horrendous hurt without furthering the hurt we feel through hate. It may sound like the weak way out, but empathy requires both emotional strength and emotional intelligence. Empathy is not a blind and reckless ambition. To empathize with those who have wronged us does not mean we agree with what they have done, justify it, or even necessarily allow that person into the personal spaces of our lives again. To empathize does not mean we lie down as a doormat or hand the person the weapon and stand still as they aim. To empathize with a person who has hurt you deeply simply means you set yourself to understand their feelings and even their experiences.

Empathy's Healing Power

If you desire healing for the soreness and injury of heartache, empathy is a precious balm. It is one of the most important tools to develop to strengthen your emotional health. We teach our children and expect others to empathize with the less fortunate, with prodigal sons and with the marginalized; but perhaps it never dawned on us that we must empathize with those who have betrayed and hurt us as well. Instead, we may think "they got what they deserved" when a person who wronged us is struck down by illness, loss, or an accident. It is human nature to want to hit back or get back. It's as old as the reptilian brain that initiates the flight or fight response. This part of our brain effortlessly leads to blasts of emotions of anger and hostility that would empty a fire extinguisher and still rage on. Also note, this part of the primitive brain is what helped cavemen survive wild animals and other dangers by triggering a cascade of stress hormones to help escape or put up a fight. However, flight or fight required speed and strength but little depth of thought. When we allow this part of our brain to respond to hurt, it takes very little thought but demands huge energy which withdraws from our emotional health account. In addition, because very little thought is involved, using this part of the brain to respond to hurt is rarely rational or the best option. Instead, the overreaction while underthinking makes skies darker than they appear at the same time creating further internal and external discord.

You may feel removed from your outward reactions that may be displayed through the punching of a wall or yelling by saying, "That really isn't who I am!" However, anger and hostility begin inwardly. They do not suddenly appear in the air and take your vocal chords hostage or pull your fist into a wall. Anger and hostility begin on the inside, creating an inner environment of enmity which, if not dealt with, may result in a less intelligent physical or verbal response courtesy of the reptilian brain. Many times, who is right and who is wrong is dependent upon whose perspective you're given. However, regardless of who is deemed right or wrong, for your own sake, what is important is how you handle it. Because God's love for us includes his desire for us to have peace, he lets us know we don't have to welcome hatred or hostility as a response to hurt. He declares, "Vengeance is mine; I will repay, saith the Lord" (Romans 12:19 KJV). That being said, if we try to defend ourselves, he will surely allow it, but we will suffer the difference in the results.

Empathy energizes our efforts toward a more compassionate and intelligent response while facilitating an inner environment of peace and understanding. It is an intentional and intelligent response toward those who may have otherwise been cursed out, cut-off, and disowned. It is a response that says: *I see what you have done and do not hate you. In fact, it is my choice to see more than what you've done—to see you and to understand at least somewhat your feelings and your circumstances. Through empathy I choose to show compassion for you by praying, forgiving, and being open and honest with you.* Empathy inspires the truth that hurt people have the tendency to hurt people and that those who are grateful to be healed are generous to supply compassion through empathy.

Empathy is a choice, just as anger is a choice. We all have within us a degree of ability to show empathy. Consider this: Would you be angry if someone punched you in the face? Now what if that someone was a six-month-old versus a twenty-six-year-old? Is your choice different? Now what if that twenty-six-year-old was your friend? Is your choice different? Now what if it was your friend in the middle of a seizure? Is your choice different? The point is, you make the choice on how to respond! Your choice is not forced. You can choose to lose it, to be bitter, resentful, or angry. Or you can choose empathy. Your peace, joy, and hope are in the same place you left them when you picked up their opposite! When you choose empathy, you exchange the fire and burnt ashes of anger for peace of mind, joyful living, and hope for humanity. You choose love when you make empathy your choice.

> **Journal Jewel:** Have you ever considered that you have a choice to be empathetic and compassionate as opposed to angry, resentful, or bitter? Consider your personal choices in the past month. How have those choices impacted your emotional well-being? Now reflect on how a different reaction would have brought a different result.

The Samaritan and the Traveler

A deficit in love for others can often be traced back to a deficit in empathy. "On one occasion an expert in the law stood up to test Jesus. 'Teacher,' he asked, 'what must I do to inherit eternal life?'" (Luke 10:25). Jesus turned the question back on the lawyer, after which the lawyer responded, "'Love the Lord your God with all your heart and with all your soul and with all your strength and with all your mind'; and, 'Love your neighbor as yourself'" (v. 27). Having answered correctly, Jesus replied, "Do this and you will live." However, in an effort to justify his lack of love for others, the lawyer asked Jesus, "And who is my neighbor?" (v. 29).

Jesus had to have read the man's heart and known he had a love problem toward Samaritans. The Samaritans were half-Jews, half-gentile, and the Jews despised them because of it. Since Jesus knew the attorney's heart, he revealed what we call the parable of the good Samaritan.

Over the centuries, countless people have learned how to behave like the good Samaritan (vv. 30–37) after numerous Bible study and Sunday school lessons. The parable highlights a truth our country and many others turn a blind eye to. That truth is that those neighbors we may have been taught to despise or look down on are our neighbors Christ has called us to love. This parable reinforces the importance of loving others in the spirit of human connectedness regardless of ethnicity, socioeconomic status, or creed.

We have been taught what to do to be the good Samaritan. However, it is learning how to handle being the beat up, wounded, looked over, passed by, and left for dead traveler without losing faith and becoming bitter that's the real challenge. I imagine the traveler in the parable lying by the side of the road half dead and thinking about his life. I have never heard someone with a near-death experience say, "I thought I was going to die, and all I could think was I hate the person who did this to me." Generally, the accounts of surviving near-death experiences, including violent and nearly fatal assaults, involve the victim instead saying, "All I could think about was my children" or "I asked God for forgiveness for my sins" or "My life flashed before my eyes." They didn't harbor thoughts of hate toward others but concern for themselves and those they love.

Let's circle back to the lawyer who asked Jesus, "Who is my neighbor?" When he died, I am certain hate toward Samaritans nor hatred toward anyone else was on his mind. In the end, our thoughts are not what others have done to us, but what we have done and who we love that matter to us. Hate is the last thing any rational person thinks of when dying. So why should it be for the living? Perhaps it is because we assume we have so much time left to continue living that we resist forgiving and stew in bitterness. When that assumption is abruptly ended, hate dissipates and love for the ones who we leave behind and repentance are the two things we consider the most in our last moments.

Because the traveler in the parable was not Jesus, he could not be perfect. No traveler is. When we are wronged to such a degree that it causes emotional pain, it is always possible to see our own imperfections and sinfulness magnified in the perpetrator. As painful as it was to be knocked over, looked over, and walked over, every traveler should understand "But by the grace of God I am what I am" (1 Corinthians 15:10). Different circumstances in life could have made the traveler the robber and the robber the traveler.

The pain of being rejected, abused, or misused is not lessened by the realization that we are imperfect, but our imperfections do create a common ground with all of humanity and facilitate empathy. We are all travelers, and in some sense we have also been robbers. In chapter 9, I emphasized that we have all experienced painful hurts from others as we travel through this world, and we have all intentionally or unintentionally been the cause of painful hurt toward others. From introspection to deliberate extrospection, the traveler can seek to understand the circumstances and feelings of those who wronged and looked over him or her. The more we all make a concerted effort to empathize with our neighbor as we travel through this life, the less others will be looked over and passed by. The less others are looked over and passed by, the fewer will be the abusers and robbers.

> **Journal Jewel:** Consider the statement "The more we all make a concerted effort to empathize with our neighbor as we travel through this life, the less others will be looked over and passed by. The less others are looked over and passed by, the fewer will be the abusers and robbers." How does this make each of us a potential world changer?

The Embodiment of Empathy

Who better to introduce human connectedness than the embodiment of empathy, Jesus the Christ? Two criminals hung on either side of the Holy One. One of the criminals hanging next to Jesus attempted to persuade him to save the day, saying, "Aren't you the Messiah? Save yourself and us" (Luke 23:39). The dying man could not comprehend that the death of Christ would not only save the day but would also save anyone who believes in him. Jesus dying on that cross would be his and our only opportunity for salvation. Still, the dying man was partly right: Jesus could have saved himself. But if he had stopped the pain and stepped down off of that cross, he could not have saved us. In the hour of his death, this man could not comprehend that truth. But notice he is not preoccupied with hate for those who testified against him or those who hung him; he is too busy trying to live, pleading "Save yourself and us!"

Likewise, the penitent criminal hanging on the other side of Jesus did not complain to Christ about his upbringing, his resentments, or how much he hated those who crucified him. It was imminent death that caused an otherwise reckless man to acknowledge God and his sins, which brought about his salvation. It took seeing death to change his perspective on what mattered the most. How is it that the living waste precious time with hate while the dying are busy appreciating life and living?

All three hung in the same place but in very different situations. Only one was guiltless, but all three could have expressed at least bitterness for those who crucified them. Many of my preaching friends and I have enthusiastically asked the congregation in the middle of a sermon to "turn and tell your neighbor!" These three men hanging on crosses were neighbors too. They were close enough to "turn and tell their neighbor" anything they desired in their last moments. As for the two criminals, this may have been the only time in their lives that anyone looked past their sins to truly see them as a neighbor.

I'm so grateful Jesus would not have himself to be a stranger to any of us regardless of where we are in our age or stage of life. Christ became our neighbor. "For we do not have a high priest who is unable to empathize with our weaknesses, but we have one who has been tempted in every way, just as we are—yet he did not sin" (Hebrews 4:15).

Jesus's empathy exhibited the greatest love mankind has ever known. "God demonstrates his own love for us in this: While we were still sinners, Christ died for us" (Romans 5:8). Talk about empathy! Truly this is good news! This is the saving gospel with love and empathy at its core.

I am thankful for the good Samaritans who make tribulation bearable, but the greatest encouragers are the travelers who have experienced physical and emotional trauma and have done the emotional hard work of pressing past primitive responses to arrive at and thrive in empathy. This emotional rite of passage creates good travelers who bless, encourage, lift up, and help heal other travelers. Once you have been the traveler, being the good Samaritan is beyond a command. It is an honor and a privilege.

Father, I come before you, not for myself, but for those who have harmed me. Initially, the pain clouded my thought life, bringing resentment and bitterness. But tugging at my heart throughout the battle between vengeance and your voice was your love. It warmed the coldness that crept in through the cracks of my shattered heart. It then mended the broken pieces and helped me see the betrayer through your eyes as one in need of grace and mercy just as I am.

Father, I ask you to release that grace upon the one who hurt me. I pray that you would lavish the most relentless and boldness of grace that frees them from all emotional, spiritual, and physical bondage. I know that you are able because you have freed me and are continuing to free me.

Lord, I thank you for this gift of love that you have given me and for enabling me to share it with others. In the precious name of Jesus, I pray, amen.

Acknowledgments

To my parents, evangelist Betty Jones and elder Marcus Jones, your prayers have carried me, your wisdom has settled me, and your love has grounded me. Thank you for the unceasing well of prayer and support throughout my life.

About the Author

Stacey McDonald is a practicing school psychologist, evangelist, motivational speaker, and former lead pastor of ten years. Not only has she trained ministers for leadership, equipping them for ministerial success in and out of the pulpit, she has also been pivotal in strengthening businesses by teaching teams how to handle toxic stress before stress handles them. Stacey has provided biblical counseling to families, couples, and youth resulting in healthy minds and healthy homes. From sharing in the lives of her congregants to counseling students and supporting families, Stacey has been touched by the resiliency of humankind.

Stacey not only hosts weekly live streamed mental health empowerment sessions, but her passion for mental health also birthed the podcast *The Gospel of Mental Health*, which provides guided relaxation, meditation, and teaching sessions on various leading podcast platforms. The infinite potential born from pain is nothing short of miraculous, and to be a midwife to such encouraged her writing of *The Gospel of Mental Health: From Mental Hell to Mental Wellness*.

Stacey lives in Lexington, Kentucky with her husband where they have reared three children and are the proud grandparents of a vivacious three-year-old granddaughter. You can learn more about Stacey at www.mcdonaldministries.org.

Endnotes

1   See, for example, Lynette L. Craft and Frank M.
Perna, "The Benefits of Exercise for the Clinically
Depressed," *The Primary Care Companion to the
Journal of Clinical Psychiatry* 6, no. 3 (2004):
104–111, https://www.ncbi.nlm.nih.gov/pmc/articles/
PMC474733/.

2   Genesis 25:18–24.

3   Genesis 22:8 NKJV.

4   Genesis 25:28.

5   Genesis 31:40–41.

6   Genesis 25:28.

7   2 Timothy 2:19.

8   Matthew 10:30.

9   Hebrews 12:2.

10 Yang Claire Yang, Courtney Boen, Karen Gerken,
Ting Li Kristen Schorpp, and Kathleen Mullan
Harris, "Social Relationships and Physiological
Determinants of Longevity across the Human Life
Span," *Proceedings of the National Academy of Sci-
ences* 113, no. 3 (January 4, 2016): 578–83, https://

www.pnas.org/content/113/3/578; Harvard Health Publishing, "Strengthen Relationships for Longer, Healthier Life," Harvard Medical School, January 18, 2011, https://www.health.harvard.edu/healthbeat/ strengthen-relationships-for-longer-healthier-life.

11 Johnson Oatman Jr., "Blessings," 1897.

A free ebook edition
is available with the
purchase of this book.

To claim your free ebook edition:

1. Visit MorganJamesBOGO.com
2. Sign your name CLEARLY in the space
3. Complete the form and submit a photo of the entire copyright page
4. You or your friend can download the ebook to your preferred device

Morgan James BOGO™

A **FREE** ebook edition is available for you or a friend with the purchase of this print book.

CLEARLY SIGN YOUR NAME ABOVE

Instructions to claim your free ebook edition:
1. Visit MorganJamesBOGO.com
2. Sign your name CLEARLY in the space above
3. Complete the form and submit a photo of this entire page
4. You or your friend can download the ebook to your preferred device

Print & Digital Together Forever.

Snap a photo   Free ebook   Read anywhere